STAFFING AT-RISK SCHOOL DISTRICTS IN TEXAS

IN TEXAS

Problems and Prospects

SHEILA NATARAJ KIRBY

SCOTT NAFTEL

MARK BERENDS

Supported by the
U.S. Department of Education

RAND
EDUCATION

The research reported here was supported by the U.S. Department of Education, Office of Educational Research and Improvement's Field Initiated Studies Grant Program under Grant No. R306F60175.

Library of Congress Cataloging-in-Publication Data

Kirby, Sheila Nataraj, 1946- .
    Staffing at-risk school districts in Texas : problems and prospects /
Sheila Nataraj Kirby, Scott Naftel, Mark Berends.
        p.   cm.
    "MR-1083-EDU."
    Includes bibliographical references.
    ISBN 0-8330-2760-3
    1. Minority teachers—Supply and demand—Texas longitudinal
studies.   2. Children of minorities—Education—Texas
longitudinal studies.   I. Naftel, Scott, 1952- . II. Berends,
Mark, 1962- . III. RAND Corporation. IV. Title.
LB2833.3.T4K57 1999
331.12 ' 313711 ' 009764—dc21   99-39615
                                                                CIP

Published 1999 by RAND
1700 Main Street, P.O. Box 2138, Santa Monica, CA 90407-2138
1333 H St., N.W., Washington, D.C. 20005-4707
RAND URL: http://www.rand.org/
To order RAND documents or to obtain additional information,
contact Distribution Services: Telephone: (310) 451-7002;
Fax: (310) 451-6915; Internet: order@rand.org

PREFACE

The research reported here was supported by Grant No. R306F60175 from the U.S. Department of Education, Office of Educational Research and Improvement's Field Initiated Studies Grant Program. Teacher supply and demand issues are of critical importance as our society enters the 21st century. Over the next decade, we will need about two million new teachers, largely because of a dramatic increase in enrollments and high attrition rates as an aging teacher workforce becomes eligible for retirement. It is important to understand where these teachers will come from and where they will teach as our society faces increasing racial, ethnic, and linguistic diversity. Amidst this diversity is a continuing concern that some racial/ethnic groups are disproportionately placed at risk. The larger project focuses on teachers of at-risk children, with special emphasis on the supply and demand patterns of minority teachers, who tend to be the ones primarily teaching in high-risk districts. This report analyzes longitudinal data on teachers from Texas between 1979 and 1996 to address this issue. Our results show that although Texas has been successful in attracting minority teachers, it has a long way to go in attaining the goal of the Texas State Board of Education: to have a teacher workforce that reflects the racial/ethnic composition of the state. These results should be of interest to researchers and policymakers dealing with issues of teacher supply and demand, particularly with respect to minority teachers.

CONTENTS

Preface   iii

Figures   vii

Tables   xi

Summary   xiii

Acknowledgments   xix

Chapter One
  INTRODUCTION   1
  Staffing At-Risk Districts   2
  Research Questions   4
  Rationale for Selecting Texas as the Focus of Study   4
    Availability of Longitudinal Teacher and District Data . .   5
    High Representation of Minorities in the Teaching
      Force   5
    Commitment to Increased Diversity in the Teaching
      Force   5
  What This Report Does and Does Not Do   6
  Organization of the Report   7

Chapter Two
  STUDENTS AND TEACHERS IN AT-RISK SETTINGS   9
  Defining "At-Risk"   9
  Students in At-Risk Districts   12
    Trends in Student Enrollment   12
    Increase in the Number of At-Risk Districts   13
    Demographic Composition   16
  Who's Teaching in High-Risk Districts?   16

Chapter Three
    COMPONENTS OF TEACHER SUPPLY 19
    All Teachers 20
    Sources of Supply 23
        Continuing Teachers 23
        New Teachers 24
        Who Is in the Teacher Pipeline? 26
        Other Sources of Supply 28
    Teachers in At-Risk Districts 29

Chapter Four
    COMPONENTS OF TEACHER DEMAND 35
    Changes in Student Enrollment 35
    Patterns of Attrition 36
    Demand for New Teacher Hires 38
    Patterns of Attrition: New Teachers 39
        Methodology 39
        Results 41
        Median Survival Times for Selected Groups of
            Teachers 51

Chapter Five
    CONCLUSIONS AND POLICY IMPLICATIONS 63

Appendix
    A. Resources and Working Conditions in Low-, Medium-,
        and High-Risk Districts 67

    B. Results of Multivariate Models Based on Teacher
        Characteristics, 1980–81 to 1995–96 75

REFERENCES 79

FIGURES

S.1. Racial/Ethnic Composition of Students in Low-,
      Medium-, and High-Risk Districts, 1995–96   xv
S.2. Race/Ethnicity of Teachers in Low-, Medium-, and
      High-Risk Districts, 1995–96   xvi
2.1. Percentage of Students Passing All Achievement
      Tests, in Low-, Medium-, and High-Risk Districts,
      1995–96   11
2.2. Racial/Ethnic Composition of Students, 1980–81 to
      1995–96   13
2.3. Number of Low-, Medium-, and High-Risk Districts,
      1984–85 to 1995–96   14
2.4. Student Enrollment in Low-, Medium-, and High-Risk
      Districts, 1984–85 to 1995–96   14
2.5. Percentage of Students Economically Disadvantaged
      in Different Types of Communities, 1990–91 and
      1995–96   15
2.6. Racial/Ethnic Composition of Students in Low-,
      Medium-, and High-Risk Districts, 1995–96   16
2.7. Racial/Ethnic Composition of Teachers in Low-,
      Medium-, and High-Risk Districts, 1995–96   17
3.1. Number of Full-Time Teachers in Texas, 1980–81 to
      1995–96   20
3.2. Black/Hispanic Teachers as a Proportion of All
      Teachers, 1980–81 to 1995–96   22
3.3. Black/Hispanic Teachers as a Proportion of New
      Teachers, 1980–81 to 1995–96   26
3.4. Teachers with Permits in Low-, Medium-, and High-
      Risk Districts, 1989–90 and 1995–96   31

3.5. New Teachers Without a Degree in Low-, Medium-,
      and High-Risk Districts, 1987–88 to 1995–96   32
3.6. Teachers with Fewer Than Five Years of Experience in
      Low-, Medium-, and High-Risk Districts, 1995–96   . . .   33
4.1. Annual Attrition, All Teachers, 1980–81 to 1995–96 . . .   36
4.2. Annual Attrition by Age of Teachers, Selected Years . .   37
4.3. Total Number of New Hires and New Teachers,
      1980–81 to 1995–96   38
4.4. Cumulative Attrition from Teaching, Combined
      Cohorts.   42
4.5. Annual Attrition from Teaching, by Entry Cohort   43
4.6. Annual Attrition from Teaching of Combined Cohorts,
      by Age at Entry   44
4.7. Annual Attrition from Teaching of Combined Cohorts,
      by Subject Area   45
4.8. Cumulative Attrition from Teaching of Combined
      Cohorts, by Gender: Non-Hispanic White
      Teachers   47
4.9. Cumulative Attrition from Teaching of Combined
      Cohorts, by Gender: Black Teachers   47
4.10. Cumulative Attrition from Teaching of Combined
      Cohorts, by Gender: Hispanic Teachers   48
4.11. Annual Attrition from Teaching of Non-Hispanic
      White Teachers, Grouped Entry Cohorts   50
4.12. Annual Attrition from Teaching of Black Teachers,
      Grouped Entry Cohorts   50
4.13. Annual Attrition from Teaching of Hispanic Teachers,
      Grouped Entry Cohorts   51
4.14. Annual Attrition from Teaching of Combined Cohorts
      in Low-, Medium-, and High-Risk Districts   52
A.1. Taxable Property Value per Pupil in Low-, Medium-,
      and High-Risk Districts, 1995–96   68
A.2. Sources of Total Revenue per Pupil in Low-, Medium-,
      and High-Risk Districts, 1995–96   68
A.3. Instructional Expenditures per Pupil in Low-,
      Medium-, and High-Risk Districts, 1995–96   69
A.4. Percentage of Instructional Expenditures on Bilingual
      and Compensatory Programs in Low-, Medium-, and
      High-Risk Districts, 1995–96   70

A.5. New Teacher Salaries in Low-, Medium-, and High-
     Risk Districts, 1980–81 to 1995–96   71
A.6. Student/Teacher Ratios in Low-, Medium-, and
     High-Risk Districts, 1995–96   72
A.7. Teachers and Aides as a Percentage of Total District
     Staff in Low-, Medium-, and High-Risk Districts,
     1995–96   73

3.1. Profile of Texas Teachers, by Selected Characteristics and Years 21

3.2. Profile of New Teachers, by Selected Characteristics and Years 25

4.1. Median Survival Time in Years for Selected Groups .. 52

4.2. Means and Standard Deviations of Analysis Variables, 1987–88 to 1995–96 55

4.3. Multiplicative Factor Estimates for Cox Regression on Time to Attrition from Teaching, with District Variables, 1987–88 to 1995–96 56

4.4. Multiplicative Factor Estimates for Cox Regression on Time to Attrition from Teaching, with Race/Ethnicity and Risk Interactions, 1987–88 to 1995–96 59

4.5. Multiplicative Factor Estimates for Cox Regression on Time to Attrition from Teaching, with Race/Ethnicity and Gender Interactions, 1987–88 to 1995–96 60

B.1. Means of Analysis Variables, 1980–81 to 1995–96 76

B.2. Multiplicative Factor Estimates for Cox Regression on Time to Attrition from Teaching, 1980–81 to 1995–96 77

INTRODUCTION

Teacher supply and demand issues are of critical importance as our society enters the 21st century. Over the next decade, about two million new teachers will be needed largely because of a dramatic increase in enrollments (Gerald and Hussar, 1997) and high attrition rates as an aging teacher workforce becomes eligible for retirement (National Commission on Teaching and America's Future, 1996). It is important to understand where these teachers will come from and where they will teach. This is especially important for high-poverty districts that tend to have large numbers of students at risk of educational failure. These districts, which also tend to be disproportionately minority, are already facing difficulty recruiting and retaining qualified teachers (Lippman et al., 1996).

Given this, it is important to ask whether we will be able to staff high-risk and high-minority districts. National data show that these districts are staffed predominantly by minority teachers. Thus, the answer to the question of who will staff these districts revolves around whether we will have enough minority teachers. This report aims to fill part of this information gap by examining demand and supply of minority teachers in Texas.

RESEARCH QUESTIONS AND DATA

The two main research questions addressed in this report are:

- What defines "at-risk" districts? How do at-risk districts differ from those not at risk in terms of resources and student and teacher characteristics?

- Given that at-risk districts are staffed largely by minority teachers, what do we know about the likely future demand and supply of such teachers?

Our data consist of a longitudinal data file on public school teachers in Texas from 1979 to 1996, obtained from the Texas Education Agency. Texas is a good case study because it maintains excellent teacher personnel files and it has a large minority teaching force. These files are linked to district characteristics that allow us to define high-risk districts and the teachers who work in them.

AT-RISK DISTRICTS: STUDENTS AND TEACHERS

One objective of this research is to identify children at risk for educational failure and to examine the characteristics of the districts that serve them and the teachers who are teaching them. Prior research has shown that poverty tends to be highly correlated with lower student achievement (Berends and Koretz, in press; Grissmer et al., 1994; Hill and O'Neill, 1994). Using the percentage "economically disadvantaged" in a district, we categorized school districts as low, medium, and high risk: fewer than 40 percent, 40–59 percent, and 60 percent and higher, respectively. This categorization is highly correlated with measures of student performance.

Texas experienced a significant increase in the number and proportion of students classified as economically disadvantaged over the past 15 years and, as a result, in the number of districts serving primarily at-risk populations. We find striking differences in the racial/ethnic composition of the student body in the three risk categories (Figure S.1). In fact, Hispanics account for about 70 percent of student enrollment in high-risk districts compared with fewer than 15 percent in low-risk districts, where the school population tends to be primarily non-Hispanic white.

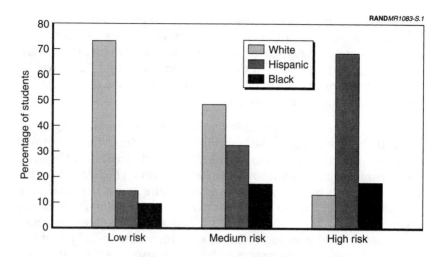

Figure S.1—Racial/Ethnic Composition of Students in Low-, Medium-,
and High-Risk Districts, 1995–96

About 37 percent of teachers teach in low-risk districts, another third
teach in medium-risk districts, and 30 percent teach in high-risk districts. However, if we examine the distribution of teachers by
race/ethnicity and by where they are teaching, we find that minority
teachers are teaching disproportionately in high-risk districts (Figure
S.2). For example, in low-risk districts, non-Hispanic white teachers
account for 95 percent of the teaching force compared with 45 percent in high-risk districts.

FINDINGS AND POLICY IMPLICATIONS

One objective of the State Board of Education is to have a teacher
workforce that reflects the racial/ethnic composition of the state
(Texas Education Agency, 1994, p. 4). However, 76 percent of all full-
time teachers are non-Hispanic white, 15 percent are Hispanic, 8
percent are black, and somewhat fewer than 1 percent are other minority. Compare this to the student body, where currently minorities
account for 54 percent of all students—37 percent are Hispanic, 14
percent are black, and 3 percent are other minority. Further, enrollment projections show that by 2025, minorities will make up two-

thirds of the student body, thus increasing the gap in representative-ness. In addition, attrition (especially among black teachers) will likely rise over the next several years because of retirements, increasing future demand. Thus, it does not seem likely that Texas will be able to hire minority teachers in sufficient numbers to make measurable progress toward its objective.

There are some disturbing implications of a potential shortage of minority teachers, particularly in high-risk districts. First, turnover in these districts will increase as new, inexperienced, non-Hispanic white teachers are hired who tend to leave at much higher rates. This turnover could potentially have adverse effects on the quality of teaching. Second, there will be increasing competition for minority teachers from other school districts within a state, from other states, and from other professions. Third, with increasing numbers of unfilled vacancies, the districts may have to resort to a number of actions to compensate for these shortages—substitute teachers, teachers from other fields, and noncertified teachers—actions that are not likely to improve the quality or continuity of teaching.

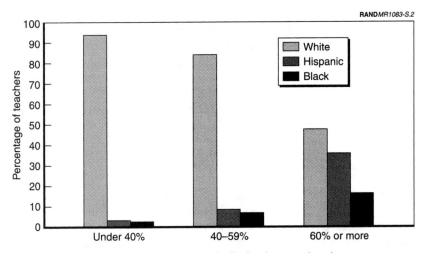

Figure S.2—Race/Ethnicity of Teachers in Low-, Medium-, and High-Risk
Districts, 1995–96

We find that minority teachers tend to have lower attrition than white, non-Hispanic teachers but that, controlling for everything else, high-risk districts experience significantly higher attrition than low-risk districts. In addition, our findings suggest that minority teachers tend to display a greater sensitivity to pay and working conditions, especially in high-risk districts. Thus, raising beginning teacher salaries, reallocating resources to increase the number of aides and support staff, or lowering the student/teacher ratio in high-risk districts may well have important payoffs in both recruiting and retention of minority teachers. Of these, raising teacher pay holds the most promise for reducing attrition. Presumably, this would not only increase teacher supply in general but may increase the supply of high-quality teachers who, because they have greater nonteaching labor market opportunities, are likely to be even more sensitive to working conditions and pay.

ACKNOWLEDGMENTS

We are grateful to Joseph Wisnowski, Coordinator for School Finance and Fiscal Analysis, Texas Education Agency, for giving us access to the data used in this report and to Scott Lewis, who helped us sort through many of the data questions. Special thanks go to our reviewers, Lionel Galway of RAND and Daniel Goldhaber of the Urban Institute, and to two anonymous referees who reviewed a shorter version of this report for *Educational Evaluation and Policy Analysis*. The report has benefited considerably from their comments in terms of both substance and clarity. Thomas Sullivan, a RAND colleague, provided helpful comments on the analysis during the course of the project. We thank Karshia Farrow for her assistance with the draft report and Patricia Bedrosian for her impeccable editing.

Chapter One

INTRODUCTION

It is no longer news that our society will be experiencing dramatic demographic changes in the next 10 to 20 years. There will be a dramatic increase in enrollments and an increasing demand for teachers within the next decade. For example, in 1996, total school enrollment in K–12 was 51.5 million. This is projected to increase to over 54.3 million by 2007 (Gerald and Hussar, 1997). The number of Hispanic children aged 5–17 years is expected to grow by a third in the next decade and to more than double by 2025, whereas the number of black children aged 5–17 years is expected to grow by a quarter by 2025 (U.S. Bureau of the Census, 1997; see also National Research Council, 1997). The next decade will also see an enormous increase in the demand for teachers (about two million) fueled by these large enrollment increases and high attrition rates as an aging teacher workforce becomes retirement-eligible (National Commission on Teaching and America's Future, 1997). Where these teachers will come from and where they will teach is a crucial issue.

An interdependent issue arises because students from minority backgrounds face both structural and individual obstacles during the schooling years that place them at risk of educational failure (Natriello et al., 1990; Wilson, 1991; Berends and Koretz, 1996 and in press). For example, they are more likely to live in households with incomes below the poverty line and have parents with limited educational attainment or limited English proficiency (U.S. Bureau of the Census, 1995). Thus, the projected change in the racial/ethnic composition of school-aged children implies a substantial increase in the size of the educationally disadvantaged population. As Natriello et al. (1990, p. 40) point out, "Failure to educate the educationally disadvantaged adequately may have catastrophic consequences for the social and economic well-being of this country." The 1996 report *What Matters Most: Teaching for America's Future*, produced by the National Commission on Teaching and America's Future (1996, p. 88), emphasized the need for high-quality teachers, especially in schools serving at-risk students:

> All schools must be adequately funded and staffed by first-rate teachers. . . . To ignore this imperative is to allow the nation to skate dangerously close to irreparably harming its public education system and its single best hope for preserving American democracy.

STAFFING AT-RISK DISTRICTS

National data show that minority teachers play an important role in staffing high-risk and high-minority districts. For example:

- In 1993–94, about 16.3 percent of all students were non-Hispanic black and 11.9 percent were Hispanic compared with 8.6 and 3.7 percent of all teachers, respectively. However, in central cities where 27.8 percent of students were black and 21 percent were Hispanic, the proportion of teachers who were black or Hispanic rose to 16.7 and 7.3 percent, respectively.

- Similarly, in public schools with 50 percent minority enrollment, minority teachers constituted 37 percent of all teachers compared with 2–7 percent in schools with 0–30 percent minority enrollment (U.S. Department of Education, 1997).

There is evidence suggesting that high-risk districts already face problems in recruiting and retaining qualified teachers (Lippman et al., 1996). These districts are seeing and will continue to see the largest increase in enrollment in the future; given the statistics above, the answer to the question of staffing is inextricably linked to the availability of minority teachers to teach in these high-risk districts.[1]

---

[1]The question being asked here is different from the question of representativeness— that is, whether the teacher population should mirror the student population, a question about which there is disagreement. Zapata (1988a, p. 19), for example, argues that attracting more minority teachers is critical because "teachers from minority backgrounds may be better prepared to meet the learning needs of an increasing pro-

In 1993–94, only 13.5 percent of the total teaching force was minority—6.7 percent black, 4.1 percent Hispanic, and 1.8 percent other minority—far less than the proportion of minority students (one-third in the public schools) (National Commission on Teaching and America's Future, 1997). The underrepresentation of minorities in teaching compared with the student body is likely to become worse over time because the proportion of minorities in teaching is declining (Task Force on Teaching as a Profession, 1986; Holmes Group, 1986; Darling-Hammond et al., 1987; Alston, 1988; Murnane and Schwinden, 1989; Feistritzer, 1990; Murnane et al., 1991; Kirby and Hudson, 1993), and this decline is likely to continue as few minorities are in the teaching pipeline (Koretz, 1990).

---

portion of the school population than teachers from other backgrounds" (see also Dilworth, 1986; Zapata, 1988b; Farrell, 1990; Ogbu, 1974, 1978, 1989, 1992; Fordham and Ogbu, 1986).

In addition, it is widely believed that minority teachers can act as mentors and role models for minority students. For example, Ogbu (1992), based on his extensive comparative research on various minority groups, suggests that the teachers who learn about the students' backgrounds, histories, and community organization can better serve the needs of high-risk students, their parents, and communities—thus overcoming some of the obstacles to their integrating into society's mainstream. Serving as mentors, teachers can also provide a buffer between the dominant culture of the school—its curriculum, instructional styles, and orientation toward the American economic structure—and the pull of high-risk students' peers and community histories (see also Ogbu, 1974, 1978, 1989; Fordham and Ogbu, 1986).

On the other hand, the evidence regarding a direct correlation between teacher diversity and student academic performance is mixed at best (Ferguson, 1991; Ehrenberg and Brewer, 1995; Ehrenberg et al., 1995). For example, Ehrenberg and Brewer, in a reanalysis of 1966 data from *Equality of Educational Opportunity*, found that after controlling for teachers' verbal scores and other characteristics, black teachers were associated with lower gains than white teachers for elementary students but higher gains for black high school students. Ehrenberg et al. (1995) found no statistically significant effects of race/ethnicity on scores for white, black, or Hispanic students using data from the 1988 National Educational Longitudinal Study. Ferguson (1991), in his detailed analysis of Texas and Alabama data, found little evidence that black teachers are significantly better than white teachers in helping black children to perform better on standardized tests. However, the differences in performance of first-graders by socioeconomic status (SES) of the teacher are intriguing: high-SES black teachers were the most effective in raising scores for white students and least effective in raising scores for black students; low-SES black teachers and high-SES white teachers were the most effective in raising black scores. Ferguson points out that black teachers usually have weaker academic preparation and lower test scores than white teachers. Given this, the fact that students do not seem to do worse on average with black teachers may point to some compensating set of skills or attitudes.

The causes for the decline are well-known and include factors such as the increasing array of alternative white-collar occupations available to minorities and the higher salaries available in many of these fields compared with teaching. In addition, researchers believe that the decline has been further exacerbated by the increasing use of standardized tests to screen entrants for teacher certification (and sometimes for entry into education programs) (Murnane and Schwinden, 1989; Murnane et al., 1991; Spellman, 1988; Kirby and Hudson, 1993). For example, Dometrius and Sigelman (1988) find that pass rates of minority teachers in Texas tend to be markedly lower than those of nonminority teachers and warn that "the imposition of teacher testing will have a homogenizing impact on the racial-ethnic diversity of the Texas educational work force, measurably decreasing the number of black and Latino teachers" (p. 81).

RESEARCH QUESTIONS

The main focus of this study is at-risk students and the resources available to them in terms of teachers and schools. The two main research questions addressed in this report are:

- What defines "at-risk" districts? How do at-risk districts differ from those not at risk in terms of resources and student and teacher characteristics?

- Given that at-risk districts are staffed largely by minority teachers, what do we know about the likely future demand and supply of such teachers?

RATIONALE FOR SELECTING TEXAS AS THE FOCUS OF STUDY

Texas was selected as the focus of study for three reasons: Texas maintains excellent teacher personnel files, it has a large minority teaching force, and it has an explicitly stated commitment to increasing diversity in its teaching force.

Availability of Longitudinal Teacher and District Data

In addition to personnel data, Texas has detailed district data as well. With the assistance and cooperation of the Texas Education Agency, we were able to match these personnel records over time to create a longitudinal data file on public school teachers in Texas from 1979–1996, obtained from the Texas Education Agency. These data provide a complete work history of teachers during this period. These files have been linked to district characteristics that allow us to define high-risk districts and the teachers who work in them. However, because district data are available only for the years 1980–1995, for most of our analyses, we are limited to this 16-year period.

High Representation of Minorities in the Teaching Force

In 1995–96, minorities constituted 24 percent of the full-time teaching workforce: Hispanics accounted for 15 percent of the teaching force, 8 percent were black, and fewer than 1 percent were other minority. In particular, the presence of a large Hispanic teaching force offers a unique opportunity to study the career patterns of Hispanics. This is particularly important because with some exceptions (notably recent research carried out by the Texas Education Agency, 1994, 1996), there is little systematic, longitudinal, large-scale research aimed specifically at Hispanic teachers.

Commitment to Increased Diversity in the Teaching Force

Texas is also an important case study because a stated objective of the State Board of Education is to have a teaching force that reflects the ethnic composition of the state (Texas Education Agency, 1994, p. 2). The Education Agency provides three reasons for adopting this objective:

- Students need role models of people in professional positions who are like them; the absence of role models sends a negative signal that minorities cannot aspire to such positions.

- Teachers may interact more successfully with students who share similar cultural backgrounds. The report cites studies that show (a) white teachers are more likely to assign Hispanic students to special education classes than white students at the same level of achievement; and (b) Hispanic teachers are less likely to mistake language problems as learning disabilities.[2]

• Diversity in the teaching force may foster knowledge and understanding of different cultures on the part of all teachers.

WHAT THIS REPORT DOES AND DOES NOT DO

It is important to be clear about what this report does and does not do. We piece together evidence from a variety of data sources and analyses—including a detailed analysis of teacher attrition—about the likely future demand and supply of minority teachers. However, given the limitations of our data, we cannot address the question of teacher quality in high-risk districts directly. This is an important limitation because a growing body of literature suggests that teacher quality can have a significant effect on student outcomes. For instance, detailed studies of teacher ability and qualifications have found that teacher preparation in mathematics and science has a positive effect on student achievement in those subjects (Monk and King, 1994; Goldhaber and Brewer, 1997a, 1997b). Additionally, there is evidence that teachers' cognitive ability serves as an important predictor of how effective a teacher will be in the classroom. For instance, individuals who score higher on standardized exams and attend more selective colleges tend to be more effective teachers as reflected in student outcomes (Ehrenberg and Brewer, 1994; Ferguson, 1991, 1998; Strauss and Sawyer, 1986).

In fact, recent research provides strong evidence that teacher quality is the single most important school factor affecting student achievement. Sanders and Horn (1994) find that the effectiveness of teachers has a larger effect on students than any other school factor and that there is a wide range of performance among teachers. However, it appears that the most important teacher attributes are difficult to identify in extant data. For instance, the ability of teachers to convey knowledge or their enthusiasm for class material might have a dramatic effect on students, but these characteristics are difficult to quantify in data and may not be related to identifiable characteristics that are more easily measured (Goldhaber et al., 1999).

---

[2]The report does not provide any references to these studies.

Thus, although teacher quality is a central issue, as we said above, our data do not allow us to address this issue. We have some measures of teacher quality: percentage of uncertified teachers teaching in at-risk districts, proportion of teachers with no degrees, and teaching experience, but these are proxies at best. The evidence we gather is suggestive and informative but a great deal more work remains to be done in this area.

ORGANIZATION OF THE REPORT

This report is organized around the themes of teacher supply and teacher demand, with particular emphasis on minority teachers and at-risk school districts. The second chapter provides some background data on Texas and provides a rationale for our measure of "risk" and how we use this to categorize districts as high-, medium-, and low-risk districts in terms of the proportion of students at risk for educational failure. The third chapter examines the components of teacher supply, using a variety of data sources. The fourth chapter delineates the components of teacher demand, the most important of which is teacher attrition. The major focus of this chapter is, therefore, an examination of teacher attrition patterns, which encompasses both bivariate and multivariate analyses. Conclusions are presented in the final chapter. Appendix A presents data comparing low-, medium-, and high-risk districts along a variety of dimensions. Appendix B presents an alternative specification of the multivariate model of teacher attrition, using the full span of data, 1980–81 to 1995–96. Although the report does not attempt to construct a full-scale teacher demand and supply model, the evidence presented here on the separate components of teacher demand and supply offers interesting, provocative, and troubling insights into the future demand and supply of minority teachers.

Chapter Two

STUDENTS AND TEACHERS IN AT-RISK SETTINGS

In this chapter, we first define our measure of risk and then use this measure to characterize school districts as low, medium, and high risk. We present a profile of students who are being served by these at-risk districts and of their teachers.

DEFINING "AT-RISK"

One of the two main objectives of the report is to examine the characteristics of the districts who serve large numbers of students at risk of educational failure. To do so, we need to identify what constitutes high risk for educational failure. Prior research has shown that poverty tends to be highly correlated with lower student achievement (Berends and Koretz, in press; Grissmer et al., 1994; Hill and O'Neill, 1994). Texas district data included a variable called "percent economically disadvantaged," which encompassed all those eligible for free or reduced-price meals under the National School Lunch and Child Nutrition Program as well as those eligible for other forms of public assistance. Children who come from families with incomes below 185 percent of the poverty level ($30,433 for a family of four in 1998) are eligible for reduced-price meals and as such would be included in this measure. We based our definition of risk on this measure and categorized school districts as low, medium, and high risk based on the percentage economically disadvantaged in the district: fewer than 40 percent, 40–59 percent, and 60 percent and higher.[1]

---

[1]It might be helpful to provide some basic information about the school districts in Texas. There are over 1,000 school districts and they vary greatly in size as measured

These cutoffs, although somewhat arbitrary, were based on an analysis of the relationship between percentage economically disadvantaged and student achievement, measured by the number of students passing all Texas Assessment of Academic Skills (TAAS) tests they attempted as a percentage of the total number of students who took one or more tests. This measure includes all students tested in grades 3 through 8 and 10 in reading and mathematics, and grades 4, 8, and 10 in writing.[2]

We find that in 1995–96, three-quarters of students in the low-risk category passed all tests, compared with 65 percent in the medium-risk districts and 56 percent in districts classified as high risk.[3] Figure 2.1 shows the boxplots for the percentage passing all tests for the three categories of districts. Boxplots provide information about the center, spread, and symmetry of a distribution and are especially valuable when comparing two or more distributions.[4] The middle 50 percent of low-risk districts all performed better than the middle 50 percent of high-risk districts. In fact, an above-average high-risk district—for example, one at the 75th percentile—has a passing rate that would place it only in the bottom 10 percent of low-risk districts. The

---

by enrollment. They range from Houston with over 200,000 students to 45 districts that have fewer than 100 students each. Most districts are rural and small, with more than 500 districts serving fewer than 1,000 students each.

[2]We did not use the percentage passing the TAAS as our measure of risk because the TAAS was introduced only in the early 1990s and we wanted a consistent, more general, descriptive measure that we could use to track changes in numbers of at-risk districts over time as well as to be crosswalked to national data.

[3]These differences are not due simply to the larger numbers of low-scoring economically disadvantaged students in high- and medium-risk districts. We find that within different categories of students, passing rates are higher in low-risk districts. For example, 61 percent of economically disadvantaged students in low-risk districts passed all tests, compared with 52 and 51 percent of these students in medium- and high-risk districts. A similar pattern of lower performance in at-risk districts was found for different racial/ethnic groups.

[4]Figure 2.1 is a box-and-whisker diagram that shows the distribution of the percentage of students passing all tests by risk category. In a box-and-whisker diagram, the line in the box is at the median value—half the schools fall above the line and half fall below. Each box captures the middle 50 percent of the schools. The lines, called whiskers, at each end of the box show the range of scores beyond the upper and lower quartiles. Outlier districts are indicated by the shaded circles. The box-and-whisker plot thus allows us to compare the centers (median or center of the box), spread (measured by the interquartile range or the height of the box), and tails of the different distributions.

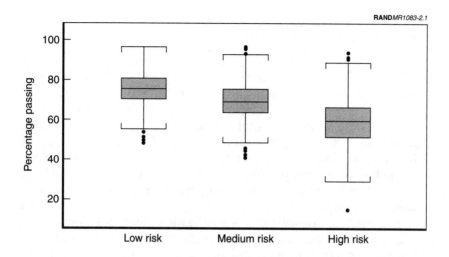

RAND*MR1083-2.1*

Figure 2.1—Percentage of Students Passing All Achievement Tests, in
Low-, Medium-, and High-Risk Districts, 1995–96

spread among high-risk districts is larger than among low-risk districts, with longer tails in the distribution.

Our measure of risk is also related to other measures of student performance. The average high-risk district has an annual dropout rate that is 50 percent higher than the average low-risk district.[5] For students who remain in school and are expected to graduate, Texas school districts keep track of college entrance test scores. Among low-risk districts, 17.4 percent of graduates scored at or above a criterion score (1,000 on the Scholastic Aptitude Test or 24 on the American College Test) whereas among high-risk districts, only 7.5 percent did so. Thus, our measure of risk—percentage economically disadvantaged—seems to track well with risk of educational failure. Students in high-risk districts have lower achievement scores on the

_____

[5]Some of the largest districts, which are urban and high risk, have the highest dropout rates. So, when looking at actual numbers of students instead of district averages, the differences between high- and low-risk districts are even greater. Though low- and high-risk districts have about the same total enrollment, high-risk districts had twice the number of dropouts in 1995–96.

TAAS, higher dropout rates, and among those who graduate, are far less likely to take and then score well on college entrance tests.

We use our measure of risk to categorize districts as low, medium, and high risk to see whether and how such districts differ in terms of characteristics that might have an effect on the quality of schooling offered in these districts. These characteristics include taxable values per pupil, sources of total revenue per pupil, instructional expenditures per pupil, beginning salaries for teachers, and student/teacher ratios as a proxy for working conditions. The results of the analysis are presented in Appendix A. The main conclusion is that there are few differences among these districts with respect to overall revenue, teacher pay, or student/teacher ratios. However, there are substantial differences among these districts in terms of the demographic composition of the student body and teacher force. The next section addresses this issue.

STUDENTS IN AT-RISK DISTRICTS

Trends in Student Enrollment

The number of students enrolled in Texas public schools has been increasing steadily since 1980–81, from 2.9 million to a little over 3.7 million, an increase of around 28 percent. The numbers of minority students and students classified as economically disadvantaged, which tend to be highly correlated, have been increasing at an even faster pace in recent years. From 1990–91 to 1995–96, the number of economically disadvantaged students rose from 1.3 million (39 percent of students) to 1.74 million (47 percent of students)—an increase of 436,000 potentially high-risk students in a five-year period. In addition, since 1990–91, minority students have become the majority, largely because of a big increase in the number of Hispanic children.

Figure 2.2 shows the racial/ethnic composition of the student body from 1980–81 to 1995–96. In 1995–96, two out of every five children in Texas schools were Hispanic. These increases in economically disadvantaged and minority students can be linked to high levels of immigration in Texas, different demographic trends among population subgroups, and economic conditions in Texas.

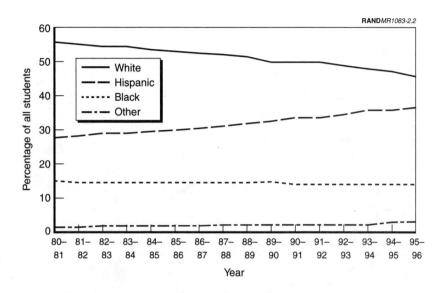

Figure 2.2—Racial/Ethnic Composition of Students, 1980–81 to 1995–96

Increase in the Number of At-Risk Districts

The number of districts classified as medium to high risk has grown substantially over time. Figure 2.3 shows that by 1995–96, of the 1,044 districts in Texas, 642 were medium or high risk. Since 1984–85, close to 300 districts classified as low risk have had increases in the number of low-income students, moving them across the threshold into the medium- or high-risk category. As the number of districts at risk has increased, the total numbers of students in these medium- and high-risk districts have more than doubled.

Figure 2.4 shows the number of students enrolled in low-, medium-, and high-risk districts since 1984–85. The districts in the three risk categories now have nearly equal total enrollment figures, despite the fact that there are only about 200 high-risk districts. This is largely because the two largest districts—Houston and Dallas—are both classified as high risk. Together medium- and high-risk districts serve about 2.3 million students.

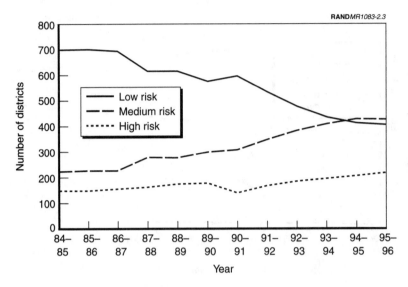

Figure 2.3—Number of Low-, Medium-, and High-Risk Districts,
1984–85 to 1995–96

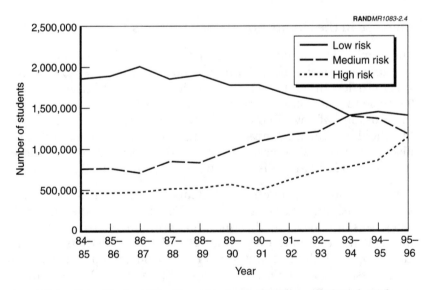

Figure 2.4—Student Enrollment in Low-, Medium-, and High-Risk
Districts, 1984–85 to 1995–96

The increase in the population of economically disadvantaged children is not limited to certain types of communities. As Figure 2.5 shows, all have experienced some increase over the five-year period. Major urban areas—defined as the largest school districts in the state, which serve the seven metropolitan areas of Houston, Dallas, San Antonio, Fort Worth, Austin, Corpus Christi, and El Paso—experienced an increase of almost 10 percent in the number of students classified as economically disadvantaged. In 1995–96, 64 percent of the over 700,000 students in these districts were classified as economically disadvantaged. About half of the students in both central cities and rural areas are classified as at risk. In contrast, major suburban districts adjacent to major urban areas (with an enrollment of over one million) had the lowest proportion of at-risk students: fewer than a third, although this was about 8 percentage points higher than the corresponding figure five years earlier.

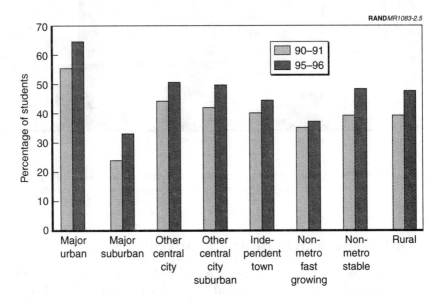

Figure 2.5—Percentage of Students Economically Disadvantaged in Different Types of Communities, 1990–91 and 1995–96

Demographic Composition

We find striking differences in the racial/ethnic composition of the student body in the three risk categories. Figure 2.6 shows clearly that both high-risk and medium-risk districts tend to have larger proportions of minorities. In fact, Hispanics account for about 70 percent of student enrollment in high-risk districts compared with less than 15 percent in low-risk districts, where the school population tends to be primarily non-Hispanic white.

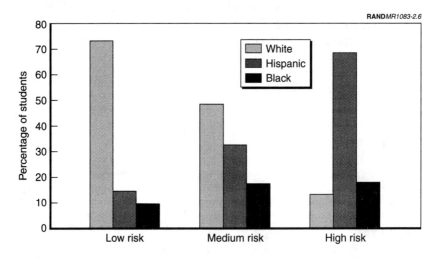

RAND*MR1083-2.6*

Figure 2.6—Racial/Ethnic Composition of Students in Low-, Medium-, and High-Risk Districts, 1995–96

WHO'S TEACHING IN HIGH-RISK DISTRICTS?

About 37 percent of teachers teach in low-risk districts, another third teach in medium-risk districts, and 30 percent teach in high-risk districts. However, if we examine the distribution of teachers by race/ethnicity and by where they are teaching, we find that minority teachers are teaching disproportionately in high-risk districts (Figure 2.7). For example, in low-risk districts, non-Hispanic white teachers account for 95 percent of the teaching force; in contrast, in high-risk districts, non-Hispanic white teachers account for less than half of all teachers. This underscores the importance of what we said above: The recruiting and retention of minority teachers, who disproportionately make up the teaching force of high-risk districts, is a crucial and urgent issue if we are not to face troubling shortages in districts that are already facing the most challenges.

We now examine the components of overall teacher supply and demand, paying special attention to minority teachers and, where data permit, to at-risk districts.

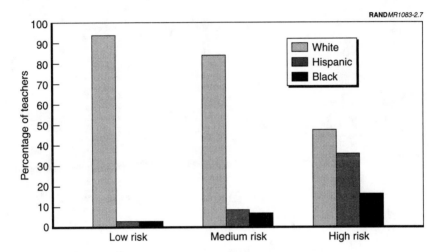

Figure 2.7—Racial/Ethnic Composition of Teachers in Low-, Medium-, and High-Risk Districts, 1995–96

Chapter Three

COMPONENTS OF TEACHER SUPPLY

The total teaching force in Texas at the beginning of any given year is composed of three groups of teachers: (1) continuing teachers who were present and teaching in the previous year, (2) new entrants into the system, and (3) returning teachers (those who were previously teaching in the Texas public school system who are now returning to teaching after a break in service) and migrating teachers (teachers who are transferring from other teaching posts in private schools or from other states). Any assessment of future supply requires information not only on current teachers but also on the teacher training pipeline (students currently in teacher education programs) and on the "reserve pool" of individuals who are qualified to teach but are not currently teaching.[1] Data on these pools of prospective teachers and their likelihood of transitioning into the teacher workforce are hard to come by and even more difficult to forecast. Haggstrom et al. (1988) suggest that we should view supply projections as "conditional estimates that depend on the numbers of prospective teachers in the populations of interest as well as factors, such as certification rules and salary levels, that affect entry rates into the teaching force" (p. 25).

---

[1]The proliferation of alternative certification programs makes the size of this pool potentially very large and increases the difficulty of assessing future supply by several orders of magnitude.

ALL TEACHERS

In 1995–96, the total number of full-time public school teachers in Texas was about 240,000, compared with 152,000 15 years earlier—an increase of 58 percent (Figure 3.1). Table 3.1 presents a profile of the teaching force for selected years by various demographic character-istics. The Texas teaching force, like those of other states, consists predominantly of women; fewer than a quarter are men, which is somewhat lower than the proportion in other states (for example, Indiana). The proportion of minority teachers has increased slightly over time but the racial/ethnic composition has undergone a dra-matic change. In 1995–96, Hispanics accounted for 15 percent of the teaching force, 8 percent were black, and fewer than 1 percent were other minority. This represented a sharp change from 1980–81 when Hispanics and blacks were equally represented in the teacher work-force, accounting for about 11 percent each (see also Figure 3.2). The average age of teachers in 1995–96 was 42 years, a marked increase

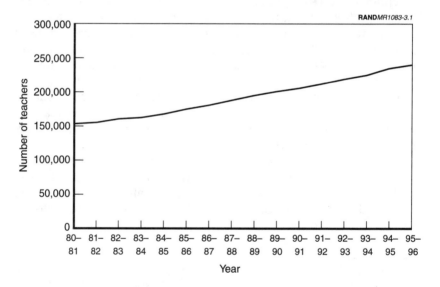

Figure 3.1—Number of Full-Time Teachers in Texas, 1980–81 to 1995–96

Table 3.1

Profile of Texas Teachers, by Selected Characteristics and Years
(in percent)

Characteristic	1980–81	1985–86	1990–91	1995–96
Sex				
Female	75.9	77.4	78.2	77.4
Male	24.1	22.6	21.8	22.6
Race/ethnicity				
Non-Hispanic white	78.2	77.5	77.7	76.1
Hispanic	10.6	12.4	13.2	15.0
Black	10.9	9.8	8.8	8.1
Age				
20–24	4.6	2.9	2.0	1.7
25–29	21.5	15.3	12.1	13.6
30–34	23.1	18.2	14.4	12.2
35–39	17.9	20.8	17.3	13.9
40–44	12.9	16.3	20.1	16.7
45–49	10.4	11.0	14.9	18.5
50–54	6.5	8.4	9.6	12.9
55+	3.1	7.2	9.6	10.5
Years of teaching experience				
0	5.2	5.7	6.1	6.1
1–4	25.3	19.9	19.0	22.3
5–8	22.1	20.5	17.8	15.2
9–12	16.5	18.1	16.3	13.9
13–16	11.0	13.9	14.4	12.3
17–20	7.5	9.1	11.5	11.3
21–24	5.3	5.7	7.3	9.1
25+	7.1	7.1	7.7	9.8
Primary teaching assignment				
Nondepartmental (elementary)	40.5	45.5	52.9	50.3
Special education	9.9	9.7	7.3	7.1
English	8.3	9.1	8.7	8.4
Mathematics	5.8	6.2	6.4	6.2
Physics/chemistry	0.4	0.5	0.6	0.7
Biology	1.2	1.5	2.4	1.8
Other science	2.2	3.0	2.0	2.3
Other departmental	31.7	24.5	21.5	23.2
Continuing/returning/new				
Continuing teachers	85.4	85.2	88.0	89.4
Returning teachers	9.7	9.4	6.7	5.1
New teachers	5.0	5.6	5.5	5.5
Number	152,091	174,696	205,530	239,331

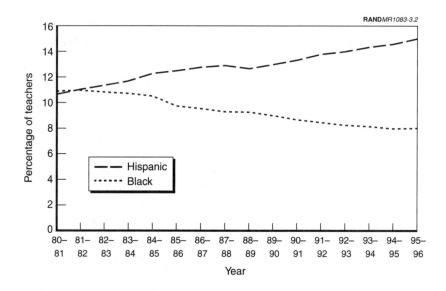

**Figure 3.2—Black/Hispanic Teachers as a Proportion of All Teachers,
1980–81 to 1995–96**

from 16 years earlier when the average age was 36 years. The gradual
aging of the teacher force is evident in the table: In 1980–81, only
one in five teachers was 45 years or older; by 1995–96, over two in
every five teachers were 45 years or older.[2] This aging of the teacher
workforce implies that the demand for new teachers is likely to increase dramatically in 10–15 years as a spate of retirements hits the
public school system.

This aging is matched by an increase in experience. By 1995–96, almost 20 percent of teachers had over 20 years of experience compared with 16 years earlier, when this group accounted for only 12
percent of the force.

About half the teachers teach at the elementary (nondepartmental)
level. The proportion of elementary teachers increased by 13

_____

[2]The aging of the workforce is even more pronounced among black teachers, who are
likely to be retiring at disproportionate rates over the next 5 to 15 years. Twenty-nine
percent of black teachers are now over the age of 50.

percentage points over the 1980 decade[3] but seems to have declined modestly since then as the baby boomlet makes its way through the school system. Unlike what we see in other states, the proportion of special education teachers has actually declined from a high of 10 percent in 1980–81 to a little over 7 percent in 1995–96. The increase in other departmental teachers seen since 1990–91 is primarily due to the increase in bilingual teachers. A recent report on educator demand and supply in Texas reported that the number of bilingual/English as a second language teachers increased by 52 percent between 1989–90 and 1993–94, teachers of gifted programs by 32 percent, followed by foreign language (21 percent), total science (19 percent), and special education (18 percent) (Southern Regional Education Board, 1996).

SOURCES OF SUPPLY

Continuing Teachers

The composition of the teaching force—continuing teachers (defined as returning/migrating teachers, or new, beginning teachers—has important implications for teacher supply and demand.

We find that the proportion of continuing teachers has increased sharply over time, from 85 percent in 1980–81 to 89 percent in 1995–96. In the absence of increasing enrollments or change in educational policies, this would decrease teacher demand. Returning teachers are an important source of supply but over time have declined in importance as a source of new hires. The fact that teachers (both in Texas and the nation as a whole) are tending to continue in teaching in higher proportions suggests that the traditional reserve pool of teachers (the pool of trained, experienced teachers who take a break from teaching and then return) may be much smaller in the future; this is supported by the fact that new, beginning teachers are accounting for a much larger share of new teacher supply. This is true across the nation as well. Data from the Schools and Staffing

---

[3]This may be partially due to the state-mandated law passed in 1985 regarding class size. State law required a student/teacher ratio of 25:1. The actual average in K–2 in 1985 was 27:1. By 1988, the K–2 number was reduced to 20–21 students per teacher. The large increase in the proportion of elementary teachers is due partly to this mandate and partly to increased enrollments.

Surveys (SASS) show that both public and private schools are hiring proportionately more first-time teachers than reentrants and transfers. In 1991, new teachers accounted for 42 percent of all hires, compared with only 31 percent in 1988.

New Teachers

 The importance of new teachers as a source of supply is underscored by the fact that they currently account for over half of all hires compared with only a third in 1980–81.[4] The size of this cohort has increased dramatically over time, from about 7,600 in 1980–81 to over 13,000 in 1995–96, an increase of over 70 percent.

Table 3.2 presents a profile of beginning teachers for selected entry cohorts. The proportion of men varies over time but has substantially increased in recent years; in 1995–96, they accounted for about 30 percent of the new teacher cohort.

The racial/ethnic composition of new teacher cohorts shows that Texas has been able to attract increasing numbers of minorities in recent years (Figure 3.3). In 1995–96, minorities represented 26 percent of the new teacher cohort compared with 23 percent of all teachers. Although the Texas report on Teacher Diversity and Recruitment (Texas Education Agency, 1994) points to the low number of black teachers in the state and writes that this is "of particular concern because African Americans are joining the teaching force in smaller and smaller numbers" (p. 25), the last two years have seen an increase in the proportion of new teachers who are black. In addition, the trends with regard to Hispanic recruitment and retention appear to be even more positive. Hispanics currently account for 18 percent of new teachers, compared with 12 percent in 1988–89, whereas blacks constitute 9 percent. Texas has undertaken a serious effort to recruit and retain minority teachers (Texas Education Agency, 1994), and it deserves credit for a great deal of success in these areas.

New teachers are entering teaching at older ages. Over time, the average age of new teachers has increased from 27.7 to 31 years.

---

[4]This is true across the nation as well.

Table 3.2

Profile of New Teachers, by Selected Characteristics and Years
(in percent)

Characteristic	1980–81	1985–86	1990–91	1995–96
Sex				
Female	76.3	81.2	77.5	70.2
Male	23.7	18.8	22.5	29.8
Race				
Non-Hispanic white	79.8	81.1	77.8	72.4
Hispanic	13.3	11.1	15.2	17.2
Black	6.5	7.5	6.3	8.9
Age				
20–24	45.0	33.0	25.0	20.9
25–29	32.2	35.9	35.5	40.3
30–34	11.1	12.5	13.1	11.7
35–39	5.6	9.8	11.3	9.3
40–44	3.2	4.9	8.7	8.4
45–49	1.7	2.4	3.6	5.5
50–54	0.8	1.1	1.5	2.3
55+	0.5	0.5	1.3	1.5
Primary teaching assignment				
Nondepartmental (elementary)	37.4	51.2	57.1	46.8
Special education	13.5	8.1	8.0	8.5
English	6.8	7.8	9.2	9.1
Mathematics	5.0	6.2	6.1	7.1
Physics/chemistry	0.2	0.3	0.4	0.5
Biology	1.0	1.8	2.5	2.3
Other science	2.9	4.6	2.5	3.0
Other departmental	33.2	20.0	14.2	22.7
Number	7,661	9,735	11,303	13,264

Whereas in 1980–81 young teachers, who were 20–24 years of age and presumably new college graduates, formed the majority of entering teachers, by 1995–96, teachers aged 25–29 years accounted for two-fifths of all beginning teachers entering teaching; well over a quarter—27 percent—were 35 years or older. This suggests either that new graduates are postponing teaching, perhaps to stay in school longer or to try other occupations, or that alternative certification programs are successfully attracting graduates from other occupations. The trend in the age distribution has important

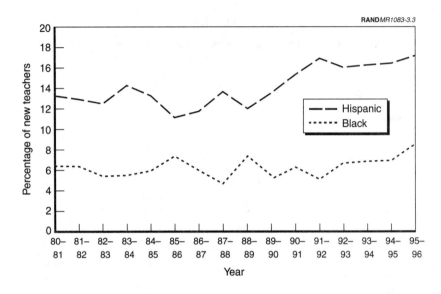

Figure 3.3—Black/Hispanic Teachers as a Proportion of New Teachers, 1980–81 to 1995–96

implications both for future supply—older teachers tend to stay in teaching thus reducing the reserve pool—and for future demand—there is a greater need to replace such teachers after comparatively short careers.

As we reported above when discussing the total teaching force, the proportion of elementary teachers increased sharply over a 10-year period to match enrollment increases and to comply with the mandate of lower class sizes. By 1990–91, about 57 percent of all beginning teachers hired were for the elementary level; this declined quite sharply by 10 percentage points to 47 percent in 1995–96 as the baby boomlet moved from elementary to secondary schools.

Who Is in the Teacher Pipeline?

However, the pipeline of new Texas teacher graduates does not look very promising. There are two major hurdles to becoming a teacher: (a) the Texas Academic Skills Program (TASP) test (instituted in 1989), which must be passed before enrolling in teacher education coursework beyond six hours; and (b) the Examination for Certification of Educators in Texas (ExCET), which must be taken even by out-of-state teachers wishing to teach in Texas. The ExCET consists of a series of subject and program-specific competency tests. The Texas study (Texas Education Agency, 1994) followed a cohort of students enrolled in the seventh grade in 1982–83 through college and students' attempts to obtain a teaching certificate. Of the original pool of over 250,000 students, fewer than 10,000 passed all the requirements to become a teacher. The major hurdles for minorities were graduation from high school and enrollment in college. For example, only about 37 percent of the original cohort of minorities enrolled in college compared with 60 percent of whites. Of these freshmen, a small percentage (12 percent of whites and Hispanics and 6 percent of blacks) applied to become teacher education majors. The TASP and the ExCET proved to be a harder barrier for minorities than for non-Hispanic whites. For example, in 1988–89, only 76 percent of Hispanic students and 66 percent of black students passed the TASP compared with over 90 percent of non-Hispanic white students. In 1991–92, 85 percent of Hispanic examinees and 72 percent of black examinees passed the ExCET compared with 95 percent of non-Hispanic white examinees. Of those newly eligible to teach, 14 percent were Hispanic and 3.2 percent were black.

In addition, a Southern Regional Education Board report (1996) offers an important snapshot of new teacher graduates as of 1990–91. Of those receiving a bachelor's degree in education that year, 77 percent were non-Hispanic white, 18 percent were Hispanic, and 4 percent were black. Only 5 percent of these were minority men (4 percent Hispanic and 1 percent black). However, not all of these individuals entered teaching. Among 1989–1991 graduates, on average, approximately 45–55 percent of all those receiving bachelor's degrees in education entered teaching within one year of graduation and about 60 percent within three years of receiving the degree; but the yield rate differs by race/ethnicity. Hispanic teachers—both male and female—tend to have the highest first-year yield rates (about 54 percent for 1991). Blacks, especially black males, have the lowest yield rates (45 percent for black females, 28 percent for black males). White females had a first-year yield rate of 52 percent in 1991 and white males had a yield rate of 39 percent.

Other Sources of Supply

Clearly, however, new teacher graduates are only one component of teacher supply in the state. In 1993–94, 51 percent of all new teachers were graduates of university-based teacher preparation programs. In addition, Alternative Certification Programs (ACPs) prepared 17 percent of new hires. The term "alternative certification" (AC) encompasses all avenues whereby an individual, not traditionally prepared in schools of education, can become licensed to teach. These avenues range from programs that place teachers with little or no training in schools to well-designed, rigorous programs aimed at individuals with subject matter knowledge. There is considerable controversy over AC programs and the quality of the teachers they prepare.[5] AC programs are diverse and widespread, but there is little empirical evidence on the effect of these programs on students, on teachers and the teacher labor

---

[5]For example, proponents of AC programs argue that they can help reduce teacher shortage problems in urban areas and in specific subject areas such as mathematics and science (Stoddart and Floden, 1995; Shen 1997); ACPs can provide greater opportunities for those with deep subject matter knowledge and enthusiasm for teaching (Kearns, 1990; Kerr, 1983; Kramer, 1991); there is little difference between these teachers and more traditionally prepared teachers in terms of knowledge or instructional practice (Ball and Wilson, 1990), or in terms of student outcomes (Goldhaber and Brewer, forthcoming); AC attracts both teachers who have "real world" labor market experiences that would serve them well in the classroom and minorities and males who may serve as role models (Cornett, 1990; Haberman, 1990; Kirby et al., 1989; Ludwig and Stapleton, 1995; Stoddard, 1992); AC can be a good source of teachers willing to teach in urban schools (Natriello and Zumwalt, 1993; Feistritzer and Chester, 1998); AC programs reduce the costs of teacher training and so lower barriers to entry which may entice high-quality individuals to enter the profession (Kirby et al., 1989; Ballou and Podgursky, 1998); AC programs help break up the virtual monopoly that university-based schools of education have had on teacher preparation and introduce competition that can force such schools to rethink and redesign their programs (Bliss, 1990; Cornett, 1990; Fenstermacher, 1990).

However, opponents of AC programs point out that some programs may result in lower professional standards allowing poorly prepared teachers into schools (Darling-Hammond, 1990, 1994; Kirby et al., 1989); AC programs start with an assumption that knowledge of subject matter is the basis of good teaching, an assumption that has been sharply criticized (Feiman-Nemser and Buchanan, 1987; Kennedy, 1991; Zeichner, 1986); several researchers have argued that pedagogical content knowledge is very important in knowing how to teach (Darling-Hammond, 1990; Gomez and Stoddart, 1991; Grossman, 1989a, 1989b; McDiarmid and Wilson, 1991; Stoddart, 1991); AC has not fulfilled its promise to bring into teaching those with higher academic qualifications (Natriello et al., 1990; Shen, 1997); and AC teachers do not have the same commitment to teaching as a career as more traditionally prepared teachers (Shen, 1997).

market, and on schools. However, given the large numbers of new teachers that will be needed over the next decade, a better understanding of the effectiveness of alternative certification programs is of central importance to improving educational outcomes, particularly in large, urban, high-poverty, high-minority school districts.

Among ACP graduates who passed the ExCET, 46 percent were minority so these programs are an important and fruitful source of supply of minority teachers.[6]

Some new teachers came from other routes (from other states, for example). These are a poor source of minority teachers in Texas (in 1991–92, only 9 percent of out-of-state teachers who passed the ExCET were minority).

Another source of supply is teachers with emergency certifications[7]; these usually form a very small proportion of new teachers but in times of perceived shortages of certified teachers, their numbers are likely to rise. We discuss this further below.

TEACHERS IN AT-RISK DISTRICTS

There are indications that high- and medium-risk districts have been facing a shortage of qualified teachers. When a teaching position cannot be filled by a candidate certified in the required field, or possibly in any field, districts must fall back on a variety of short-term measures, including issuing temporary teaching permits that allow individuals to teach without full certification.[8] Overall, these num-

---

[6]The Texas Education Agency report (1996b) on teacher preparation reports that several campus administrators expressed a preference for hiring university-trained teachers rather than ACP graduates and also suggested that ACP interns required far more support than other teachers in terms of classroom management and student discipline. However, ACP graduates were less likely to leave within the first five years than other new teachers.

[7]Sometimes these teachers are included among alternatively certified teachers.

[8]Five types of permits currently allow teaching without appropriate certification. Four are used for persons seeking the necessary certification and are issued for varying lengths of time. The fifth is issued by a district and approved by the commissioner of education. It is for degreed individuals who do not have any type of teaching credential. These permits can be used indefinitely in the issuing district.

bers are small but our data indicate that high-risk districts have been forced to rely on these noncertified teachers to a greater degree than low-risk districts as a short-term solution to a potential shortage of qualified teachers.

Figure 3.4 shows the average proportion of teachers holding permits in low-, medium-, and high-risk districts. In 1995–96, 5.6 percent of teachers had permits in the average high-risk district, compared with 3.4 percent in the average low-risk district.[9] These figures represent an improvement over 1989–90, when over 9 percent of teachers had permits in the average high-risk district. It is very likely that these percentages are higher today than in 1995–96, given the overall shortage of teachers being reported nationwide.

There are also differences among districts in the educational attainment of teachers, although there is some controversy over whether advanced degrees translate into higher quality. High-risk districts have fewer teachers with advanced degrees: 25.3 percent, compared with 29.2 percent for low-risk districts.[10] What is more troubling, however, is that high-risk districts also hire more teachers with no degree. These teachers may be career and technology teachers who are certified based on other professional qualifications, full-time substitute teachers, aides reported as teachers of record, or alternative certification interns on probationary certificates while working on full certification (Texas Education Agency, 1995). Although career and technology teachers and alternative certification interns may be good-quality, career-track hires, full-time substitutes and aides working as teachers of record are more temporary and are used only when districts are unable to fill positions with qualified, permanent teachers.

---

[9]These figures are calculated at the district level and are biased upward because of the higher percentages of teachers with permits in small districts. In 1995–96, 3.5 percent of all Texas teachers had one or more permits, compared with 4.2 percent in 1990–91.

[10]It should be noted that a relatively low proportion of teachers in Texas have advanced degrees compared with other states. Over the past decade this proportion has been steadily falling in Texas, probably reflecting the lack of an effective incentive program. In 1984–85, 36.2 percent had advanced degrees and by 1996–97 this had fallen to only 27.2 percent. The 1993–94 SASS reports that nationally 47.3 percent of teachers have advanced degrees (U.S. Department of Education, 1997).

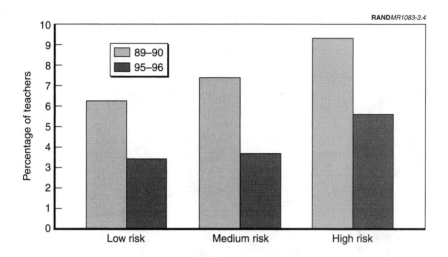

Figure 3.4—Teachers with Permits in Low-, Medium-, and High-Risk Districts, 1989–90 and 1995–96

Figure 3.5 shows the proportion of new teachers with no degree in the three risk districts since 1987–88. The percentage of nondegreed teachers has generally declined in medium- and low-risk districts over this period, but the upward trend in high-risk districts since 1991–92 is disturbing. New teachers with no degree also tend to be disproportionately minority. For example, 14 percent of black and 10 percent of Hispanic teachers hired from 1987–88 to 1995–96 had no degree, compared with only 3 percent of non-Hispanic white teachers. The evidence suggests that urban and at-risk districts that rely on the minority labor force are facing a shortage of qualified applicants who are willing to work in these districts. We find that many of the teachers without degrees do appear to be hired on a temporary basis in response to supply shortages. Evidence of this can be found in the attrition behavior of teachers without degrees. Nearly 40 percent of these teachers leave after one year, compared

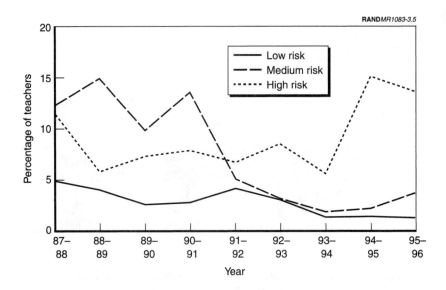

RAND*MR1083-3.5*

Figure 3.5—New Teachers Without a Degree in Low-, Medium-, and High-Risk Districts, 1987–88 to 1995–96

with 14 percent of new teachers who hold bachelor's degrees.[11] The use of teachers with no degree is most prevalent in major urban areas, where about half of all these teachers are hired.

High turnover among teachers or sharply increasing demand lead to a less experienced workforce. Experience is an important concern in teaching because performance tends to improve with experience, particularly during the first several years of a career (Murnane and Phillips, 1981a, 1981b; Hanushek et al., 1998). Compared with low- and medium-risk districts, high-risk districts on average have a higher proportion of novice teachers (Figure 3.6). Not surprisingly, teachers in high-risk districts also have a lower average level of experience—10.6 years compared with 11.7 and 11.4 in medium- and low-risk districts.

---

[11]First-year attrition rates are particularly high among new, black teachers with no degree; these teachers have a first-year attrition rate of 55 percent. Our multivariate analysis confirms that teachers with no degree have dramatically higher attrition rates, particularly black and Hispanic teachers.

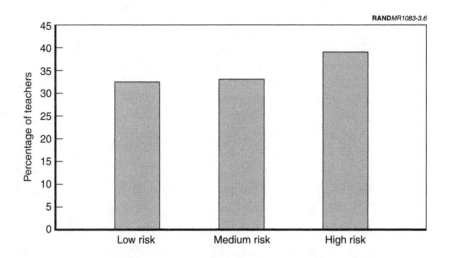

RAND*MR1083-3.6*

Figure 3.6—Teachers with Fewer Than Five Years of Experience in Low-,
Medium-, and High-Risk Districts, 1995–96

All in all, the evidence provided here paints a somewhat pessimistic
picture of teacher supply and teacher quality (as measured by certification, educational attainment, and experience) in high-risk districts. Other studies (Ferguson, 1998) also find that teacher quality is
generally lower in high-risk districts, as do national data from the
Schools and Staffing Surveys (Choy et al., 1992).

Chapter Four

COMPONENTS OF TEACHER DEMAND

Unlike teacher supply, the components of teacher demand are much more clear-cut. Teacher demand depends on enrollment growth, teacher turnover, and mandated curriculum or other policies including mandated class sizes. Teacher turnover includes losses from death, retirements, disability, and other events (either voluntary or involuntary) and is the most important component of teacher demand (Grissmer and Kirby, 1987). State policies have not changed dramatically over the late 1980s and early- to mid-1990s. Therefore, we focus on the first two components.

CHANGES IN STUDENT ENROLLMENT

Texas schools are enrolling increasingly diverse student bodies, and a larger proportion appear to be economically disadvantaged and likely to be at risk for educational failure. Currently, minorities account for 54 percent of all students: 37 percent are Hispanic, 14 percent are black, and 3 percent are other minority. Total school enrollment is projected to increase from about 3.8 million students in 1995 to 5.3 million by 2025, and the Texas Education Agency (1994) projects that by 2025, minorities will make up two-thirds of the student body. Hispanics will account for 46 percent of all school-aged children, blacks for 14 percent, and other minority for 4 percent. Similar projections are reported by other commissions as well.

PATTERNS OF ATTRITION

It is useful to examine the annual attrition rates of teachers because these are the most important component of teacher demand (along with changing enrollments and mandated student/teacher ratios) (Grissmer and Kirby, 1987).

As Figure 4.1 shows, although annual attrition rates have varied over the 16-year period, there has been a general downward trend over time. Recently, attrition has been about 10 percent a year over the last nine years compared with 11–14 percent in the early 1980s.[1]

There are some differences in attrition by race/ethnicity. Hispanics tend to have lower attrition rates of between 7 and 8 percent, although this has declined since the early 1980s as well.[2] The rate for black teachers shows a surprising spike during the 1984–86 period

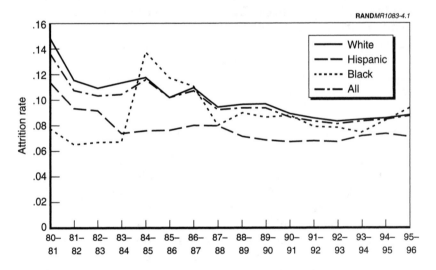

Figure 4.1—Annual Attrition, All Teachers, 1980–81 to 1995–96

---

[1]SREB (1996) reports a lower attrition rate for 1992–93 of 6.7 percent. However, its data included all teachers (full-time and part-time).

[2]For 1992–93, we had to estimate the rate for Hispanics by excluding one large district which had a large proportion of Hispanic teachers but appeared to have missing or poor quality data.

when attrition rose rather sharply. One possible and partial explanation might be the implementation of the Texas Examination of
Current Administrators and Teachers (TECAT), a test of basic literacy
given to all Texas teachers in 1986. Black teachers had much lower
passing rates (82 percent) than either Hispanics (94 percent) or non-
Hispanic whites/other minority (99 percent) and the advent of the
test may have caused some teachers to leave teaching rather than
take the test. For example, Shephard and Kreitzer (1987) cite re-
marks made by the Texas Commissioner of Education reporting that
as a result of the test, 10,000 teachers decided to leave teaching in
1987: 2,000 who failed and 8,000 who never showed up to take the
test.

Examining annual attrition is important because it indicates how
many teachers will need to be replaced in a steady state. However, it
masks variation in attrition by age. Figure 4.2 shows a U-shaped relationship between age and attrition, with the likelihood of attrition
being much higher during the early stages of the career, very low during midcareer, and high as the teacher approaches retirement. This

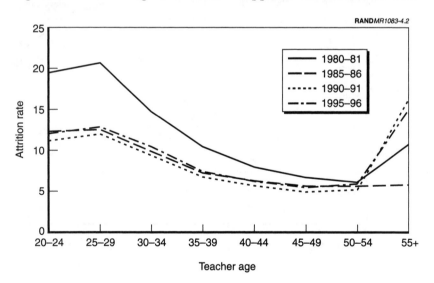

Figure 4.2—Annual Attrition by Age of Teachers, Selected Years

pattern holds true not only for a single group of teachers but for
groups of teachers over time as well, with the overall curve moving
down to reflect the decrease in attrition that we had shown above.
By and large, attrition rates have remained stable over the past 10
years. The attrition rate of young teachers is about 11–13 percent; for
those aged 40–54, the attrition rate is only 5 percent or a little higher;
and for those who are 55 and older, attrition rises sharply because of
retirement.

DEMAND FOR NEW TEACHER HIRES

Figure 4.3 shows that, on average, Texas hires about 25,000 teachers
every year of whom roughly half are new teachers, although as we
saw above, this proportion has varied considerably over time. The
sharp decrease in teacher demand in 1983–84 is surprising, given the
steady increase in student enrollments shown above. However, the
increase in the subsequent two years is likely to result from several
factors: (a) the mandated lower class size and its effect on K–2; (b)

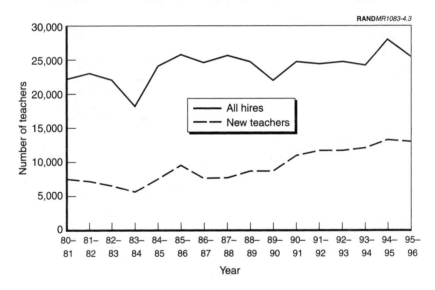

**Figure 4.3—Total Number of New Hires and New Teachers, 1980–81
to 1995–96**

the need to replace teachers affected by the TECAT; and (c) increasing enrollments at the elementary level. It is interesting to note that new teachers are filling an increasing portion of new teacher demand.

The next several sections examine patterns of attrition among new teacher cohorts. These analyses provide important information, given that demand for new teachers will rise over the next 10 to 20 years, fueled by increasing teacher retirements and increased enrollments. How long do new teachers stay in teaching? Do these patterns differ by race/ethnicity or among districts categorized by risk? What are important determinants of teacher attrition? We use both descriptive and multivariate analyses to answer these questions.

PATTERNS OF ATTRITION: NEW TEACHERS

Examining annual attrition rates for all teachers is informative but limited, and comparisons over time can be a little misleading unless we adequately account for changes in the composition of the teaching force. Tracking incoming cohorts of new teachers and examining their experience over time provide better estimates of duration as well as differences in duration by selected demographic and economic factors. That is the focus of this section.

Methodology

A distinguishing feature of our data, and most time-to-event data, is that the event—in our case, attrition from teaching—may not have occurred at the time of the analysis. That is, some teachers may not have left teaching by 1996–97, although some of them may have left later. These data are "right-censored"; we know only the amount of time that has elapsed between the time the individual entered teaching and the beginning of the academic year 1996–97 and that the individual had not left teaching by then.

We use two survival analysis techniques to study when attrition occurs (Cox, 1972; Kalbfleisch and Prentice, 1980; Marquis and Kirby, 1989). The first, called the Kaplan-Meier estimator, is a descriptive technique that allows us to look at the distribution of attrition times.

This nonparametric estimator makes no assumptions about the form of the survival function but corrects for sample losses resulting from censored observations before time t. The basic function is a plot that indicates how likely it is that the teacher will continue in teaching beyond the first year, the second year, and so on. At the beginning, 100 percent of the individuals are present in the teaching force. As time passes, they gradually leave or separate from teaching Our estimate of the cumulative survival rate—the proportion that will remain in teaching within t years—is $F(t)$; therefore, the cumulative attrition rate is $1 - F(t)$. The Kaplan-Meier estimator for different subgroups allows us to examine the distribution of attrition times for groups of interest. This reveals the gross effect of that characteristic and everything else that varies with it.

To estimate the net effect of a characteristic, controlling for other characteristics, we fit a Cox proportional hazards model. This model assumes that the attrition rate function for a teacher with characteristics given by x is: $h(t;x) = g(x) h_0(t)$, where $h_0(t)$ is the underlying attrition rate function and $g(x)$ is a function of the characteristics. In the Cox model, no assumptions are made about the underlying model and the attrition rate, $h_0(t)$, is completely unspecified. This makes it particularly attractive for our purposes because we are not so much interested in describing the shape of the function as in describing how differences in characteristics alter the likelihood of attrition. In the Cox model, one assumes that the effect of an increase in a given characteristic x is to multiply the attrition rate by a constant factor $g(x)$ so that the attrition rates for groups of individuals with different levels of x are proportional. A common form for $g(x)$ is $g(x) = \exp(bx)$, where b denotes the regression coefficients to be estimated. Here, the multiplicative effect on the attrition rate of an increase in x is given by $\exp(b)$.

A concrete example may help to illustrate this. Assume that we have a reference teacher—white female elementary school teacher—whose attrition function is given by the unspecified $h_0(t)$. For a second teacher who is similar in every way except in one characteristic (he is male), we estimate that the effect of this characteristic, $\exp(b_{male}) = 0.95$. This indicates that at any point in time, the probability of attrition among male teachers is 95 percent of the attrition of female teachers or, to put it a little differently, males have a 5 percent lower attrition rate than females.

We first present some Kaplan-Meier estimators of the attrition function before turning to the multivariate model. We limit our analysis to new, full-time teachers teaching in the Texas public school system from 1980–81 to 1995–96. Recall that new or beginning teachers are defined as those who had no prior experience teaching and were reported as having zero years of experience. A new teacher cohort is defined as a group of teachers who entered teaching in the Texas public school system in a given year.

Results

Timing of Attrition. Figure 4.4 shows the annual attrition curves for the combined new teacher cohorts from 1980–81 to 1995–96. About 16 percent of teachers entering teaching leave within the first year and about 26 percent leave within two years.[3] Two in five teachers leave teaching within the first four years and close to half of the cohort leaves teaching by the sixth year. Cumulative attrition levels off after the 12th year or so; after that point, we continue to lose teachers but at about one-half to 1 percent a year. By about the 15th year, about two-thirds of an entering cohort of teachers has had at least one break in teaching.[4]

---

[3]These rates are lower than those found by Grissmer and Kirby (1992) for the combined Indiana new teacher cohorts, but they were analyzing data from 1965 to 1982 and, as we show below, attrition has declined markedly since then.

[4]This represents *annual* or first-time attrition and measures the proportion of the teaching force in any given year that leaves during or at the end of that academic year. This is what we normally mean by attrition or turnover and measures the length of time the individual has taught continuously without a break in service. *Permanent* attrition, however, looks at all the future years for which we have data to see whether these teachers return to teaching. If they do, they are not counted as leavers in that particular year. In this definition, teachers are counted as leavers only when they leave teaching and do not return to it (during the period for which we have data). Permanent attrition rates give us a better sense of the true proportion of each cohort that is lost to teaching because they account for later returns. Permanent attrition rates tend to be between 70 and 80 percent of annual attrition rates, suggesting that 20 to 30 percent of new teachers who leave return and most appear to do so within five years (Grissmer and Kirby, 1992; Murnane et al., 1991; SREB, 1996). In the Texas data, for example, the two-year permanent attrition rate for a cohort is 18 percent compared with 26 percent annual attrition, and the four-year rate is 28 percent compared with 40 percent. By the sixth year, about 36 percent of the cohort has permanently left teaching and by the 12th year, about half has left. However, a report from the State Board for Educator Certification (SREB, 1996) provides some evidence to suggest that the return rate is lower for the most recent cohorts.

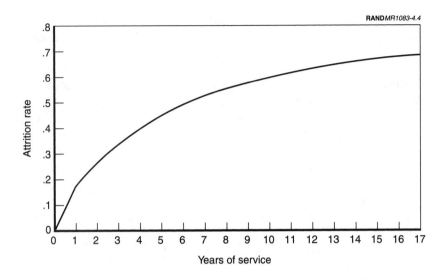

RAND*MR1083-4.4*

Figure 4.4—Cumulative Attrition from Teaching, Combined Cohorts

Attrition Differences by Cohort. Aggregating across all cohorts, although useful in providing a baseline pattern of attrition for a typical new teacher cohort, hides changes in attrition patterns over time. Figure 4.5 shows cumulative annual attrition for selected teacher cohorts: 1980–81, 1983–84, 1987–88, 1989–90, and 1991–92. It is evident that attrition has declined for the more recent cohorts but has remained quite stable since the mid-1980s. Later cohorts experience a first-year attrition of 14–16 percent compared with 20 percent for the 1980–81 cohort and a two-year attrition rate of 25–26 percent compared with 36 percent for the earlier cohort. This decline in attrition over time has been found in other states and more generally across the nation.

Attrition Differences by Age at Entry. Because the age distribution of entering cohorts has changed so dramatically over time, we thought it would be interesting to examine differences in attrition by age at entry (Figure 4.6). First-year annual attrition is much the same for the four age groups—between 14 and 16 percent (a little higher for the older teachers) but by the second year, a different pattern

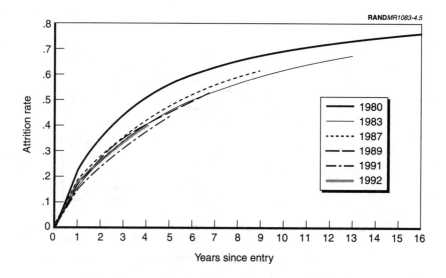

RAND*MR1083-4.5*

Figure 4.5—Annual Attrition from Teaching, by Entry Cohort

emerges. Older teachers tend to stay in teaching at much higher proportions (22 percent attrition compared with 25 percent for the less-than-30-year age group) and by the third year, the differences in attrition rates are large and significant. For example, by the fourth year, over 41 percent of the youngest teachers have left teaching compared with 32 percent of the teachers age 35 and over. By the 10th year, the difference has increased to 16 percentage points, with 65 percent of the youngest teachers leaving compared with 49 percent of the oldest teachers. Clearly, young teachers are at the greatest risk of leaving.[5]

---

[5]If we examine permanent attrition, the pattern is quite similar but the differences are not as marked, primarily because young teachers tend to return to teaching at higher rates than their older counterparts. For example, the two-year permanent attrition rate for those younger than 25 years is 15 percent compared with a first-time attrition rate of 25 percent; for teachers age 35 and older, the annual and permanent attrition rates are 16 percent and 22 percent, respectively. By the fourth year, the comparable numbers are 28 and 42 percent (age 20–24 years) and 23 and 32 percent (age 35 and over).

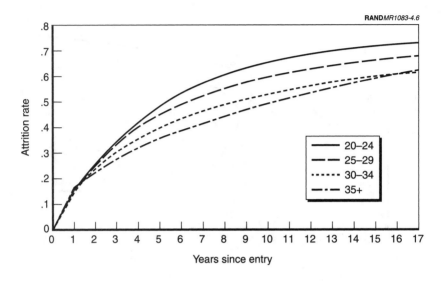

RAND*MR1083-4.6*

**Figure 4.6—Annual Attrition from Teaching of Combined Cohorts,
by Age at Entry**

Attrition Differences by Subject Area. There has been considerable
attention given to differences in attrition across subject areas: in
particular, whether mathematics and science teachers have higher
attrition rates than those teaching other specialties and whether they
tend to return less frequently. Prior research (Murnane et al., 1991;
Grissmer and Kirby, 1992) found that the highest rates of attrition are
among physics/chemistry, English, and biology teachers. This may
be partly explained by the attractive outside opportunities available
to these teachers and in the case of science teachers, poor or inade-
quate equipment and supplies that may lead them to be frustrated
and unhappy enough with working conditions to leave. Surprisingly,
mathematics teachers were found to have among the lowest rates of
attrition, along with elementary teachers. Although outside salaries
for mathematics graduates are quite high, these may be available
only to those who teach advanced courses or perhaps have a degree
in mathematics as opposed to teacher education.

Figure 4.7 portrays the cumulative annual attrition for teachers
characterized by primary assignment area (at entry) for Texas
beginning teachers. Our findings reinforce what others have found.

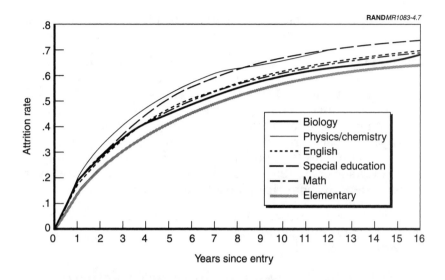

RAND*MR1083-4.7*

Figure 4.7—Annual Attrition from Teaching of Combined Cohorts, by Subject Area

Elementary teachers have the lowest attrition rates and physics/chemistry teachers have the highest attrition. By the end of the fourth year in teaching, 36 percent of elementary teachers have left, compared with 48 percent of physics/chemistry teachers. We also find that special education teachers leave at high rates equal to those of physics/chemistry teachers after the 8th year. We can offer two reasons: Either the demand has fallen off for special education teachers (we saw above that the proportion of special education teachers in the total teaching force has fallen quite sharply over time) or that special education teachers burn out after a while on the job. Unlike prior studies, we find that mathematics teachers experience higher attrition than elementary teachers: 43 percent. This difference narrows to 5 percentage points over time but remains stable over time. At the end of the 10th year, we find that 57 percent of elementary teachers, 60–61 percent of biology, English, and mathematics teachers, and 67 percent of physics/chemistry and special education teachers have had at least one break in teaching.[6]

Attrition Differences by Race/Ethnicity and Gender. Other studies have generally found that women tend to have higher annual attrition rates than men but that the differences narrow substantially when other factors (including propensity to return to teaching later) are taken into account (Grissmer and Kirby, 1992; Murnane et al., 1991). Studies also show that minority teachers tend to have much lower attrition rates than nonminority teachers (Kirby and Hudson, 1993; Murnane et al., 1991). However, there is little evidence on attrition patterns by both race/ethnicity and gender.

Figures 4.8–4.10, which show cumulative attrition rates by race/ethnicity and gender, reveal some interesting differences among the subgroups.

- We do not see the large differences in attrition between men and women that was evidenced in data from earlier periods. Women are tending to take fewer breaks from the labor force and this is reflected in the fact that their attrition rates are fairly close to those of men.

- Among non-Hispanic white teachers, we find that in the first three years, men tend to have *higher* attrition than women but this changes by the fourth year when the respective attrition rates are 40 and 41 percent. By the tenth year, the difference in attrition has increased to 4 percentage points (58 percent and 62 percent, respectively) and this difference remains stable after that point.

- Black male and non-Hispanic white female teachers have the highest attrition rates of all the groups.

- Among minority teachers, we find interesting patterns by gender. For example, unlike non-Hispanic whites, black male teachers

---

[6]When we examine permanent attrition, the attrition rates are considerably lower but the pattern remains the same. For example, the 10-year attrition rate is 45 percent for elementary teachers, 50 percent for biology, English, and mathematics teachers, 54 percent for special education teachers, and 57 percent for physics/chemistry teachers.

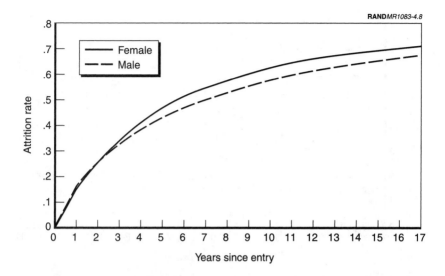

Figure 4.8—Cumulative Attrition from Teaching of Combined Cohorts, by
Gender: Non-Hispanic White Teachers

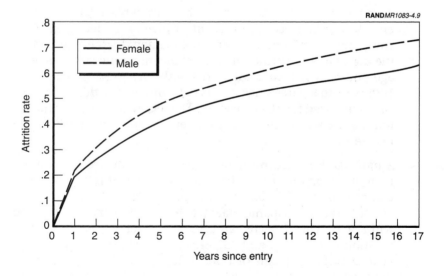

Figure 4.9—Cumulative Attrition from Teaching of Combined Cohorts, by
Gender: Black Teachers

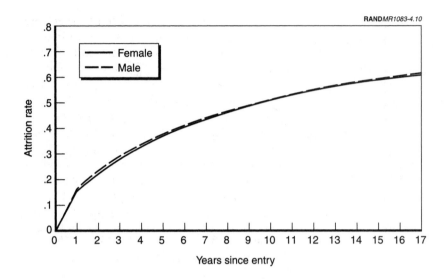

Figure 4.10—Cumulative Attrition from Teaching of Combined Cohorts, by Gender: Hispanic Teachers

have consistently higher attrition rates than black female teachers: In the first year, 24 percent of black men leave teaching compared with 20 percent of black women; by the fourth year, the difference in attrition increased to a difference of 7 percentage points (44 percent compared with 37 percent) and, by the 10th year, to 9 percentage points (62 compared with 53 percent). Given the need for black male role models in our schools, the fact that black male teachers have higher attrition than black female teachers is disturbing.

• Among Hispanic teachers, there is little or no difference between men and women. In the first five years, there is a 1 to 3 percentage point difference in attrition: For example, the two-year attrition rate of Hispanic male teachers is 25 percent compared with 22 percent for Hispanic female teachers; the four-year attrition rates are 34 and 33 percent, respectively. By the 10th year, a little over half of both groups have left teaching (51 percent).

Changes over Time. As we saw above, attrition has declined over time and we were interested in seeing whether this pattern held up for all three race/ethnic groups. We grouped our entry cohorts into three groups based on year of entry (1979–84, 1985–89, 1990–95) and examined their annual attrition patterns for the three groups separately (Figures 4.11–4.13). Among non-Hispanic white teachers, the decline in attrition over time is quite marked. For example, the four-year attrition rate declined from 49 percent for the earliest cohorts to 42 percent for those entering in 1985–89, and still further to 34 percent for the most recent cohorts. Among black teachers, however, the pattern is somewhat different: The middle years saw a significant increase in attrition. For example, the attrition rates for the 1985–89 cohorts were 9–10 percentage points higher for the first five years and then remained 3–5 percentage points higher through the 11 years for which we have data on these cohorts. The experience of the most recent cohorts is similar to that of the 1979–84 cohorts, especially after the first four years. Hispanic teachers show the same pattern of increased attrition for the middle cohorts but the most recent cohorts show somewhat lower attrition than the earliest cohorts. For example, the four-year attrition rates were 33, 37, and 31 percent for the 1979–84, 1985–89, and 1990–95 cohorts, respectively. The much higher attrition rates of the 1985–89 cohorts for black and Hispanic teachers but not for non-Hispanic white teachers suggest the existence of some policy or practice that differentially affected minority teachers but not majority teachers. One possibility is the implementation of the TECAT during this time; we have seen that minorities do not fare as well as white teachers on standardized tests. Another possibility is that particular districts—particularly those with high numbers of minority teachers—faced cutbacks in funding and so instituted reductions-in-force.

Attrition Differences by Type of School District (Low, Medium, and High Risk). As Figure 4.14 shows, the findings run somewhat contrary to our expectations. In the first three years, attrition in the high-risk districts is slightly higher than in medium- or low-risk districts by 1–3 percentage points but for later years, attrition is actually *lower* in high-risk districts. By the 10th year, for example, 60 percent of teachers working in low- to medium-risk districts have had a break in teaching compared with 56 percent of teachers working in high-risk districts. As we show in the multivariate analysis, part of this

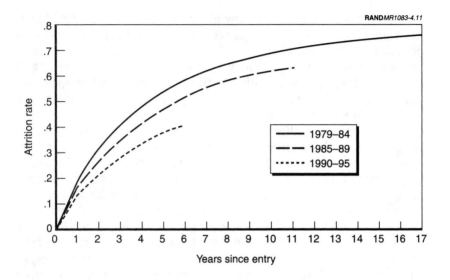

Figure 4.11—Annual Attrition from Teaching of Non-Hispanic White
Teachers, Grouped Entry Cohorts

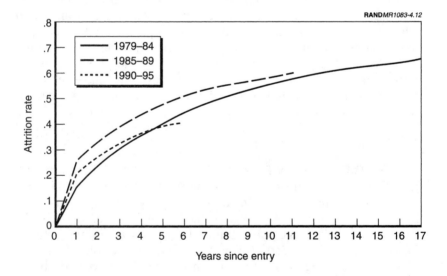

Figure 4.12—Annual Attrition from Teaching of Black Teachers, Grouped
Entry Cohorts

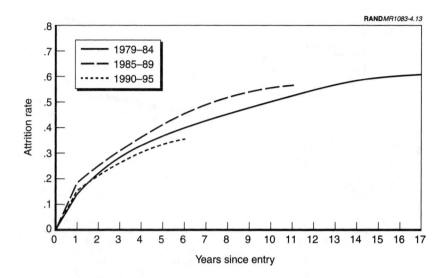

RANDMR1083-4.13

Figure 4.13—Annual Attrition from Teaching of Hispanic Teachers,
Grouped Entry Cohorts

difference is because high-risk districts are staffed largely by minority
teachers who have lower attrition than nonminority teachers.[7]

Median Survival Times for Selected Groups of Teachers

It is useful to summarize the attrition differences among the various
groups of teachers by looking at the median lifetime of a typical
teacher within that group. This statistic, which captures how rapidly
the survivor function drops (or alternatively, the cumulative attrition
function increases), represents the length of time that must pass before 50 percent of a particular group of teachers leaves teaching.

Table 4.1 shows the median survival time for typical teachers in each
of the subgroups for the annual definitions of attrition, calculated
from the descriptive functions presented above.

---

[7]There is no difference in this pattern when we look at permanent attrition, suggesting
that the propensity to return to teaching does not differ across types of districts.

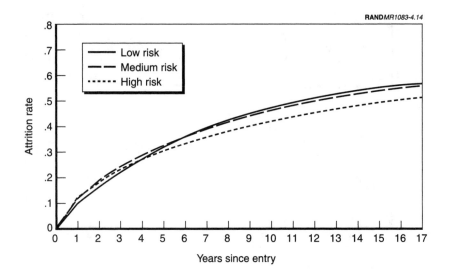

Figure 4.14—Annual Attrition from Teaching of Combined Cohorts in Low-, Medium-, and High-Risk Districts

Table 4.1

Median Survival Time in Years for Selected Groups

All cohorts	7
Gender by race/ethnicity	
Non-Hispanic white female	6
Non-Hispanic white male	7
Hispanic female	10
Hispanic male	10
Black female	9
Black male	6
Age at entry	
20–24	6
25–29	7
30–34	9
35+	11
Districts categorized by risk	
Low risk	7
Medium risk	7
High risk	8

For the combined cohorts as a whole, we find that the typical teacher will stay seven years in teaching before a break in service. Hispanic teachers (both male and female) and black female teachers have much longer median survival times (and higher return rates compared with the other groups, when one examines permanent attrition). Black male and non-Hispanic white female teachers have the shortest survival times. The large differences we saw by age at entry are quite evident here. Median survival times increase sharply with age. As we saw above, high-risk districts have somewhat longer median survival times than low- or medium-risk districts; this is largely because they tend to be staffed primarily by minority teachers, who have longer survival times.

Thus far, the graphs and table displayed here present the total effect of a characteristic and everything correlated with that characteristic rather than the net effect of that variable alone, holding all other variables constant. We present below multivariate models that estimate the net effect of each characteristic on attrition.

Multivariate Results. We estimated several different versions of the same basic model with characteristics of teachers (gender, age at entry, degree, primary teaching assignment, type of district in terms of risk category and urbanicity, race/ethnicity, beginning salary) for different cohorts of teachers. The basic conclusions are robust across the different versions, which gives us confidence in our results. The results offer interesting insights on attrition patterns of minority teachers and those teaching in high-risk districts.

The models presented here use data only from the 1987–88 to 1995–96 cohorts of new teachers because this allowed us to control for certain district variables as well.[8] For example, in addition to the teacher variables, the model controls for beginning teacher salaries, differences in student/teacher ratios, instructional expenditures per pupil, and percentage administrative and support staff, all of which can be regarded as proxies for working conditions and resources available to teachers. Another reason for using more recent data is that attrition patterns have changed markedly over the 1970s and

---

[8]The complete model, which is based on the entire 16-year period for which we have data, uses only teacher characteristics because we do not have district data for the 16-year period. The results of the complete model are presented in Appendix A.

1980s. As a result, we felt that these results are likely to be more relevant to describing relationships holding in the labor market today. In addition, the model was estimated separately for the three racial/ethnic groups: non-Hispanic whites, Hispanics, and blacks.

Table 4.2 presents the means and standard deviations of the variables used in the Cox models. Some interesting differences emerge among the three racial/ethnic groups. For example, black teachers tend to be somewhat older (a third of them are over 35) than whites or Hispanics. A higher proportion of black and Hispanic teachers do not have a college degree (10–14 percent) compared with 3 percent of non-Hispanic white teachers. Sixty percent of new Hispanic teachers are teaching in high-risk districts compared with only 15 percent of whites and 27 percent of black teachers. New black teachers are predominately teaching in medium-risk districts, whereas 50 percent of non-Hispanic white teachers are teaching in low-risk districts. There are also some noteworthy differences by the district community type where these different groups of teachers are teaching. For example, over half of all new black teachers are teaching in major urban school districts, whereas a quarter of Hispanic teachers are teaching in other central city school districts. Forty-four percent of non-Hispanic white teachers are hired into suburban school districts compared with only 31 percent of Hispanic and 26 percent of black teachers.

Table 4.3 presents the results of the estimation. Because the coefficient estimates are rather difficult to interpret, we present the multiplicative factor defined as exp(b), where b is the estimated coefficient. For the continuous variables, the multiplicative factor gives the proportional shift in the attrition rate associated with a one-unit increase in that variable (for example, a $1,000 increase in pay, a one point increase in student/teacher ratio, or a one percentage point increase in percentage administrative or professional support staff). For the other characteristics, the multiplicative factor shows the shift in the attrition rate for an individual with the particular characteristic (e.g., male) relative to that of an otherwise similar individual with the reference or omitted value for that characteristic (in this case, female). The results from the separate models largely agree, so in the discussion we focus on the results from the total model although we point out differences where they exist.

Table 4.2

Means and Standard Deviations of Analysis Variables, 1987–88 to 1995–96

Characteristic	All	Non-Hispanic White	Hispanic	Black
Sample size	98,951	76,160	15,338	6,502
Teacher pay ($1,000)	23.85 (3.2)	23.82 (3.1)	23.72 (3.5)	24.49 (4.2)
Student teacher ratio	16.15 (1.9)	16.01 (1.9)	16.52 (1.5)	16.8 (1.3)
Instructional expenditures per pupil ($1,000)	2.43 (0.8)	2.40 (0.8)	2.51 (0.8)	2.50 (0.7)
% administrative staff	3.95 (1.2)	4.08 (1.2)	3.48 (1.0)	3.62 (0.9)
% professional support staff	5.94 (1.9)	5.81 (1.9)	6.15 (1.7)	6.94 (1.5)
Gender				
Female	0.75	0.77	0.70	0.72
Male	0.25	0.23	0.30	0.28
Age at entry				
20–24	0.27	0.30	0.20	0.18
25–29	0.36	0.35	0.40	0.31
30–34	0.12	0.11	0.16	0.17
35+	0.25	0.24	0.24	0.34
Degree				
BA	0.89	0.91	0.87	0.77
MA or Ph.D.	0.06	0.06	0.03	0.09
None	0.05	0.03	0.10	0.14
Primary teaching assignment				
Nondepartmental (elementary)	0.54	0.53	0.62	0.53
Special education	0.08	0.08	0.06	0.11
English	0.09	0.09	0.08	0.07
Mathematics	0.07	0.07	0.05	0.07
Physics/chemistry	0.004	0.005	0.003	0.002
Biology	0.02	0.03	0.02	0.02
Other departmental	0.20	0.20	0.17	0.20
District educational risk				
Low	0.41	0.50	0.11	0.18
Medium	0.36	0.35	0.29	0.55
High	0.23	0.15	0.60	0.27
District community type				
Major urban	0.20	0.15	0.27	0.57
Other central city	0.14	0.12	0.24	0.09
Suburban fast growing	0.22	0.24	0.21	0.12
Suburban stable	0.18	0.20	0.10	0.14
Nonmetro with 1000+ ADA	0.14	0.15	0.12	0.06
Nonmetro with town	0.05	0.06	0.02	0.01
Rural	0.07	0.08	0.04	0.01
Race/ethnicity				
Non-Hispanic white	0.78	—	—	—
Hispanic	0.15	—	—	—
Black	0.07	—	—	—

Table 4.3

Multiplicative Factor Estimates for Cox Regression on Time to Attrition from Teaching, with District Variables, 1987–88 to 1995–96

Characteristic	All	Non-Hispanic White	Hispanic	Black
Teacher pay ($1,000)	0.971**	0.993**	0.937**	0.948**
Student teacher ratio	1.033**	1.027**	1.040**	1.072**
Instructional expenditures per pupil ($1,000)	0.926**	0.934**	0.874**	0.908**
% administrative staff	1.044**	1.042**	1.040*	1.059*
% professional support staff	0.984**	0.985**	0.979*	0.912**
Gender				
Female	*1.0*	*1.0*	*1.0*	*1.0*
Male	0.979	0.948**	0.982	1.103*
Age at entry				
20–24	*1.0*	*1.0*	*1.0*	*1.0*
25–29	0.775**	0.806**	0.770**	0.596**
30–34	0.668**	0.678**	0.733**	0.604**
35+	0.633**	0.613**	0.789**	0.631**
Degree				
BA	*1.0*	*1.0*	*1.0*	*1.0*
MA or Ph.D.	1.493**	1.478**	1.564**	1.364**
None	1.751**	1.507**	1.597**	2.350**
Primary teaching assignment				
Nondepartmental (elementary)	*1.0*	*1.0*	*1.0*	*1.0*
Special education	1.178**	1.183**	1.224**	1.134
English	1.184**	1.167**	1.335**	1.221**
Mathematics	1.238**	1.233**	1.232**	1.493**
Physics/chemistry	1.452**	1.563**	1.098	0.751
Biology	1.170**	1.152**	1.342**	1.214
Other departmental	1.131**	1.112**	1.214**	1.144*
District educational risk				
Low	*1.0*	*1.0*	*1.0*	*1.0*
Medium	1.064**	1.069**	1.017	0.964
High	1.148**	1.247**	0.888*	1.033
District community type				
Major urban	1.240**	1.234**	1.134*	1.356**
Other central city	1.037	1.069**	0.954	1.304**
Suburban fast growing	0.991	1.002	0.815**	1.118
Suburban stable	*1.0*	*1.0*	*1.0*	*1.0*
Nonmetro with 1000+ ADA	0.861**	0.885**	0.812**	1.163
Nonmetro with town	0.810**	0.838**	0.813	1.168
Rural	0.925**	0.957	0.948	1.302
Race/ethnicity				
Non-Hispanic white	*1.0*	—	—	—
Hispanic	0.838**	—	—	—
Black	1.018	—	—	—

NOTE: For each variable, the omitted or reference group is given in italics.

* Significant at the .05 level.

**Significant at the .01 level.

Although in the overall model males and females have similar attrition rates, we find interesting differences in the submodels: White males have attrition rates that are 5 percent lower than those of white females but black males have 10 percent higher attrition rates than comparable black females. As we found above in the simple bivariate results, older teachers have significantly lower attrition rates (20–40 percent lower) than younger teachers. Those with advanced degrees at entry tend to have considerably higher attrition rates than those entering with a bachelor's degree, suggesting that these teachers may have greater opportunities in the nonteaching labor market. All departmental teachers have higher attrition than elementary teachers; this has been found in several previous studies. In particular, the much higher attrition rates of science teachers is worth noting.

For this report, the racial/ethnic results and those pertaining to districts categorized by risk are the most important. Controlling for other variables, we find that Hispanic teachers have attrition rates that are about 16 percent lower than comparable white teachers but that there is no difference in the attrition rates of black and white teachers. Although our results in the bivariate analysis were mixed with respect to attrition patterns in districts categorized by risk, here we find a clearer indication that controlling for other variables, attrition is about 15 percent higher in high-risk districts. The differences across the different racial/ethnic models are interesting. Whites in high-risk districts have much higher attrition rates (almost 25 percent higher) than those in low-risk districts. This contrasts sharply with Hispanics in high-risk districts, who have about a 10 percent *lower* attrition rate than those teaching in low-risk districts, and black teachers, who show no difference in attrition across the three types of districts.

In general, central cities and major urban districts have higher attrition than suburban districts or nonmetropolitan areas.

Increases in pay significantly lower attrition, especially among Hispanic and black teachers. The multiplicative factors for pay show that a $1,000 increase in beginning salary reduces attrition by about 2.9 percent in the overall model and by 5–6 percent in the Hispanic and black models.

An increase in student/teacher ratios has a detrimental effect on attrition; an increase of one point (say from 16.15 to 17.15) would increase attrition by 3.3 percent in the overall model, and 4–7 percent in the Hispanic and black models. An increase of $1,000 in instructional expenditures per pupil (a very large increase) would reduce attrition by about 7–13 percent. An increase of 1 percentage point in administrative staff would increase attrition by 4–6 percent, whereas an increase of 1 percentage point in professional support staff would lower attrition by 2–9 percent.

It is interesting to note that the separate models indicate that minority teachers are particularly sensitive to working conditions as proxied by these variables. This is not surprising, given that they are working under what are likely to be rather difficult and underresourced conditions.

Tables 4.4–4.5 present two other versions of the full model. Here, instead of estimating separate models for each racial/ethnic group, we allow for interactions between race/ethnicity and risk and race/ethnicity and gender to see whether and how these differ. Because the other results mostly mirror the model with all teachers discussed above, we focus on the results of the interaction terms. Somewhat surprisingly, compared with non-Hispanic whites teaching in low-risk districts, blacks in low-risk districts have significantly *higher* attrition—about 12 percent higher. Compared to whites teaching in low-risk districts, whites in medium-risk districts have a 6 percent higher attrition rate, whereas those teaching in high-risk districts have a considerably higher attrition rate: 23 percent higher. Blacks have significantly higher attrition rates than whites teaching in low-risk districts, regardless of where they are teaching. Hispanics, on the other hand, have attrition rates similar to those of non-Hispanic whites in low- and medium-risk districts but Hispanics teaching in high-risk districts have much *lower* attrition (about 10 percent lower) than non-Hispanic whites in low-risk districts, a finding that offers some promise for these districts faced with high attrition among non-Hispanic teachers.

Table 4.5 underscores what we found above in the survival function results. Controlling for other characteristics, we find that black male teachers have significantly higher attrition than non-Hispanic white female teachers (13 percent higher), whereas every other group (with

Table 4.4

Multiplicative Factor Estimates for Cox Regression on Time to Attrition from Teaching, with Race/Ethnicity and Risk Interactions, 1987–88 to 1995–96

Characteristic	All
Teacher pay ($1,000)	0.971**
Student teacher ratio	1.034**
Instructional expenditures per pupil ($1,000)	0.926**
% administrative staff	1.044**
% professional support staff	0.984**
Gender	
Female	*1.0*
Male	0.978
Age at entry	
20–24	*1.0*
25–29	0.775**
30–34	0.666**
35+	0.632**
Degree	
BA	*1.0*
MA or Ph.D.	1.493**
None	1.770**
Primary teaching assignment	
Nondepartmental (elementary)	*1.0*
Special education	1.181**
English	1.185**
Mathematics	1.241**
Physics/chemistry	1.454**
Biology	1.171**
Other departmental	1.131**
District risk category and race/ethnicity interactions	
Low-risk*non-Hispanic white	*1.0*
Low-risk*Hispanic	0.982
Low-risk*black	1.124*
Medium-risk*non-Hispanic white	1.063**
Medium-risk*Hispanic	1.001
Medium-risk*black	1.075*
High-risk*non-Hispanic white	1.230**
High-risk*Hispanic	0.894**
High-risk*black	1.176**
District community type	
Major urban	1.226**
Other central city	1.047*
Suburban fast growing	0.993
Suburban stable	*1.0*
Nonmetro with 1000+ ADA	0.862**
Nonmetro with town	0.813**
Rural	0.932**

NOTE: For each variable, the omitted or reference group is given in italics.

*Significant at the .05 level.

**Significant at the .01 level.

Table 4.5

Multiplicative Factor Estimates for Cox Regression on Time to Attrition from Teaching, with Race/Ethnicity and Gender Interactions, 1987–88 to 1995–96

Characteristic	All
Teacher pay ($1,000)	0.971**
Student teacher ratio	1.033**
Instructional expenditures per pupil ($1,000)	0.925**
% administrative staff	1.044**
% professional support staff	0.984**
Gender	
Non-Hispanic white female	*1.0*
Non-Hispanic white male	0.953**
Hispanic female	0.828**
Hispanic male	0.827**
Black female	0.957
Black male	1.132**
Age at entry	
20–24	*1.0*
25–29	0.771**
30–34	0.670**
35+	0.634**
Degree	
BA	*1.0*
MA or Ph.D.	1.494**
None	1.749**
Primary teaching assignment	
Nondepartmental (elementary)	*1.0*
Special education	1.179**
English	1.185**
Mathematics	1.240**
Physics/chemistry	1.464**
Biology	1.174**
Other departmental	1.134**
District educational risk	
Low	*1.0*
Medium	1.066**
High	1.149**
District community type	
Major urban	1.240**
Other central city	1.037*
Suburban fast growing	0.991
Suburban stable	*1.0*
Nonmetro with 1000+ ADA	0.862**
Nonmetro with town	0.811**
Rural	0.926**

NOTE: For each variable, the omitted or reference group is given in italics.

*Significant at the .05 level.

**Significant at the .01 level.

the exception of black females) has significantly lower attrition, even white males. Hispanics, regardless of gender, have attrition rates that are markedly lower than those of white female teachers.

We also estimated separate models for low-, medium-, and high-risk districts as well as separate models by race/ethnicity within each of these risk categories. These models largely bear out what we saw above. Overall, teachers in high-risk districts are more sensitive to pay (a $1,000 increase in pay reduces attrition in these districts by 6.2 percent compared with 1 percent in low-risk districts and 1.6 percent in medium-risk districts) and minority teachers, regardless of type of district, are more sensitive to pay than white teachers. Although the attrition of all teachers is affected by working conditions, in high-risk districts, we find that black teachers appear to be particularly sensitive to student/teacher ratios and the presence of support staff. Unlike Hispanic teachers and black teachers, white teachers seem to react more to the district community type. For example, in high-risk districts, attrition of white teachers is 23 percent higher in both central city schools and rural schools than in suburban stable school districts.

Chapter Five

CONCLUSIONS AND POLICY IMPLICATIONS

Taken together, the evidence presented above regarding student enrollment, the increase in numbers of students at risk of educational failure, the Texas teaching force, and the entering cohorts of new teachers provides a useful and important picture of the future demand for and supply of minority teachers. Although the lessons learned from Texas may not apply generally, they should prove useful to states or school districts that face a growing minority student population and a small or declining population of minority teachers.

One objective of the State Board of Education is to have a teacher workforce that reflects the racial/ethnic composition of the state (Texas Education Agency, 1994, p. 4). Texas still has a long way to go to reach its goal. Currently, 76 percent of all full-time teachers are non-Hispanic white, 15 percent are Hispanic, 8 percent are black, and somewhat fewer than 1 percent other minority. Compare this to the student body, where currently minorities account for 54 percent of all students—37 percent are Hispanic, 14 percent are black, and 3 percent are other minority. Texas has done very well in attracting minorities to teaching using a variety of sources: In recent years, minorities have accounted for 26 percent of new teacher cohorts. Alternative Certification Programs, designed for those with bachelor's degrees in fields other than teaching, are a particularly rich source of supply. Almost half of ACP interns tend to be minority. However, as we pointed out above, there is considerable controversy over AC programs and the quality of their teacher graduates. There is clearly a need to understand this source of supply better to see how effective and committed AC teachers are.

Future supply looks less promising. There is a decreasing number of teachers in the pipeline and the mandated teacher entry and certification tests, the TASP and the ExCET, both appear to be a bigger hurdle for minorities than for white teacher candidates.

Consider the future: Enrollment projections show that by 2025, minorities will make up two-thirds of the student body. We have also seen that minorities tend to be disproportionately economically disadvantaged and, therefore, disproportionately at risk of educational failure. Thus, on top of the increase that Texas has already experienced in the early 1990s, Texas is likely to be faced with a further substantial increase in the proportion of at-risk children. In addition, attrition (especially among black teachers) will rise over the next several years because of retirements, increasing future demand. This suggests that unless Texas is successful in attracting larger numbers of black teachers, the already low representation of black teachers in the force will decline still further as these teachers retire. Nor does it seem likely, given the enormous increase in Hispanic and other minority children and attendant increase in demand for minority teachers, that Texas will be able to hire minority teachers in sufficient numbers to make measurable progress toward its objective.

There are some disturbing implications of a potential shortage of minority teachers, particularly in districts with large proportions of educationally disadvantaged students. First, if minorities are underrepresented in the new teacher graduate pool, and minorities, as we have seen, tend to teach in high-minority or high-risk districts, turnover in these districts will increase as new, inexperienced, non-Hispanic white teachers are hired, who tend to leave at much higher rates. Further, there is evidence to show that teachers make large gains in effectiveness in their first years in the classroom (Murnane and Phillips, 1981a, 1981b; Hanushek et al., 1998). Thus, turnover will likely have adverse effects on the quality of teaching.

Second, there will be increasing competition for minority teachers from other school districts within a state, from other states, and from other professions. Therefore, it will become more difficult to recruit and retain minority teachers in specific districts.

Third, with increasing numbers of unfilled vacancies, the districts may have to resort to a number of actions to compensate for these shortages. National data from the Schools and Staffing Surveys suggest that administrators in urban schools with high minority enrollments tended to use substitute teachers or assigned teachers from other fields more frequently than administrators of suburban schools—actions that are not likely to improve the quality or continuity of teaching (Choy et al., 1992). The data we have presented show that the high-risk districts in Texas tend to have higher numbers of teachers who are not fully certified or teachers with no degrees. Reinforcing this, data released by the State Board for Educator Certification (SBEC) show that in 1996–97, the proportion of noncertified teachers was much higher in urban and rural school districts than in suburban districts.[1] For example, 31 percent of rural secondary mathematics teachers and 23 percent of urban mathematics teachers were not certified compared with only 17 percent of suburban mathematics teachers. Similar differences were found among teachers of other subjects as well, including English, science, and social studies.

The one largely unanswered question—apart from the few indications above—relates to the quality of the majority of teachers in these districts. It is important that the students most in need of help be taught by teachers who are fully trained, prepared to teach, dedicated, and of high quality. If the minorities who enter teaching and stay in high-risk districts are of lower quality than those who teach in low-risk districts, in terms of test scores, academic achievement, certification status, or preparation—*and these characteristics have an adverse effect on student achievement*—then merely ensuring a supply of minority teachers to staff high-risk districts is not enough. For example, Ferguson (1998) suggests that the minority gap in student achievement in at-risk districts may be due predominantly to the lower quality of minority teachers in these districts. Overall, the literature is mixed with respect to the relationship between teacher characteristics and student performance. The issue of teacher quality is not an issue we address here.

---

[1]Teachers at grades 7–12 designated as "noncertified" include all persons assigned to or teaching outside their field of certification, persons who do not hold any type of certificate, and persons who are teaching under emergency certificates (SBEC, 1998).

Our findings suggest that minority teachers tend to display a greater sensitivity to pay and working conditions, especially in high-risk districts. Calculating rough measures of elasticity for each of these variables allows us to examine the tradeoffs among these variables in terms of their effect on attrition. The elasticity for pay ranges from 0.7 in the overall model to 1.2–1.4 in the minority models; that is, a 10 percent change in pay ($2,400, given a beginning salary of approximately $24,000) would decrease attrition by 7 percent for all teachers and by 12–14 percent for minority teachers. Elasticities for student/teacher ratios are 0.5–1.1; for instructional expenditures, 0.2–0.3; for percentage administrative staff, 0.2; and for percentage support staff, 0.1–0.5. Given these numbers, it appears that teachers are very responsive to pay and student/teacher ratios, especially minority teachers. Lowering student/teacher ratios can be very expensive and difficult to push through the bureaucracy. Such a move can often lead to unintended consequences—witness the big increase in number of uncertified teachers in California following a mandated class-size reduction, as districts scrambled to hire more teachers to comply with the mandate. However, these kinds of tradeoffs are best studied in a resource allocation framework that could provide credible estimates of relative costs of alternative policies.

Increasing teacher pay seems to hold the most promise in reducing teacher attrition, at least in terms of these results. This suggests that raising beginning teacher salaries in high-risk districts by offering signing bonuses to fully certified teachers and starting teachers who agree to teach in these districts on a higher step of the salary scale may well have an important payoff in both recruiting and retention of minority teachers. Indeed, some jurisdictions have adopted similar policies usually aimed at specific subjects. Presumably, these policies would not only increase teacher supply in general but may well increase the supply of high-quality teachers, who are likely to have greater nonteaching labor market opportunities and thus are likely to be even more sensitive to working conditions and pay.

RESOURCES AND WORKING CONDITIONS IN LOW-, MEDIUM-, AND HIGH-RISK DISTRICTS

Comparisons between low-, medium-, and high-risk districts along a variety of dimensions are presented in this appendix. Given that students in at-risk districts have much poorer educational outcomes than students in low-risk districts, it is important to examine whether the districts serving them differ in terms of available resources and working conditions as proxied by class size and number of aides.

REVENUE AND PER PUPIL SPENDING

The three types of districts vary considerably with respect to revenues and expenditures. As one would expect, high-risk districts with high percentages of economically disadvantaged students on average have much weaker tax bases than low-risk districts. Figure A.1 clearly shows this pattern in district per pupil taxable property values.[1]

The weaker tax base for poorer districts translates into lower per pupil revenues from local sources, as seen in Figure A.2, which shows revenue from all sources: local, state, and federal. However, high- and medium-risk districts, on average, have slightly more total revenue per student when state and federal sources are included. High-risk districts get more federal funds because of programs aimed at special needs or low-income students, such as the National School

---

[1]This is the district's total taxable property value, as determined by the Comptroller's Property Tax Division, divided by the total number of students in the district.

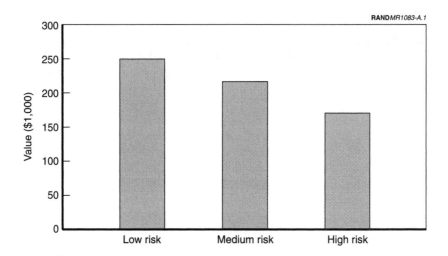

Figure A.1—Taxable Property Value per Pupil in Low-, Medium-, and High-Risk Districts, 1995–96

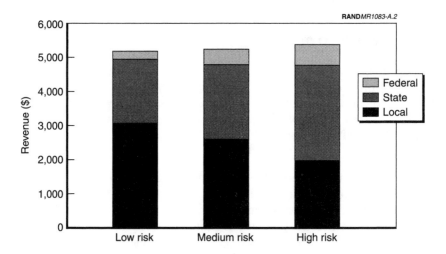

Figure A.2—Sources of Total Revenue per Pupil in Low-, Medium-, and High-Risk Districts, 1995–96

Lunch Program and Title 1 of the Improving America's Schools Act. In Texas, some state funds are also provided to districts for compensatory education programs based on enrollment of low-income students. The largest differences in district funding are related to the Foundation School Program—a system of formulas for distributing state funds that is aimed in part at equalizing funding across the districts in Texas. This finance system was developed in response to a series of legal challenges that began in 1984 with *Edgewood v. Kirby*.[2] The net result of this system is that districts least able to raise school funds locally are given sufficient state funding to bring them into approximate parity with more wealthy districts.

As we see from Figure A.3, instructional expenditures per pupil are higher in at-risk districts than in low-risk districts. This is largely due to the higher costs of educating special needs students and higher

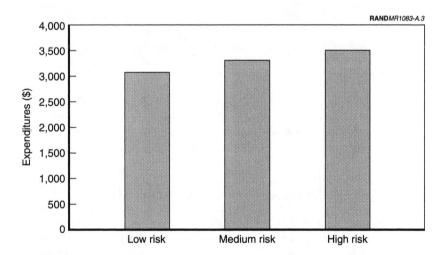

Figure A.3—Instructional Expenditures per Pupil in Low-, Medium-, and High-Risk Districts, 1995–96

---

[2]*Edgewood v. Kirby*, 94-0152, 1995, State Supreme Court of Texas. An explanation of the school finance system can be found in Texas Education Agency (1996a).

prices for inputs, including teachers.[3]   For example, as shown in Figure A.4, high-risk districts allocate 20 percent of their instructional expenditures for bilingual and compensatory programs, reflecting the needs of their largely low-income and Hispanic student body. Low-risk districts, on the other hand, spend only half of that for these programs.

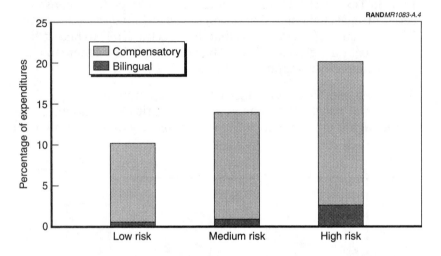

Figure A.4—Percentage of Instructional Expenditures on Bilingual and
Compensatory Programs in Low-, Medium-, and High-Risk
Districts, 1995–96

TEACHER SALARIES AND WORKING CONDITIONS

The primary focus of our study centers on teachers of at-risk students. We examine some characteristics of districts—such as pay and working conditions, as proxied by class size—to see whether and how they differ across the three risk categories.

Figure A.5 displays new teacher salaries in the three types of districts for selected years in constant 1996 dollars. At the beginning of our

---

[3]Good sources for comparisons of school district funding and costs are U.S. Department of Education (1998, 1995).

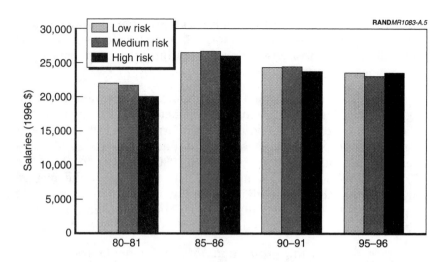

Figure A.5—New Teacher Salaries in Low-, Medium-, and High-Risk Districts, 1980–81 to 1995–96

study period, 1980–81, new teachers in high-risk districts were paid on average $2,000, or 10 percent, less than teachers in other districts. By the mid-1980s, the base salary levels of all teachers had increased significantly and teachers in high-risk districts had achieved near parity with the others. The general salary increases of the early 1980s were part of a major statewide reform effort. Along with increased salary levels, class sizes were significantly reduced, particularly in early elementary grades. These policies were enacted along with other policies designed to raise the quality of the teaching force. All teachers and administrators were required to pass competency tests (Texas Examination of Current Administrators and Teachers or TECAT) and new teachers were required to pass tests when entering, and again when completing teacher preparation programs (currently TASP (Texas Academic Skills Program), and ExCET (Examination for Certification of Educators in Texas)). Also, incentive pay supplements were instituted based on evaluations of performance and placement on a career ladder pay schedule. This policy was later discontinued, largely because of difficulties in measuring teacher performance.

As seen in Figure A.5, beginning teacher salaries have eroded some-what since the mid-1980s, by about 11 percent. However, there is little difference in salaries offered beginning teachers among the three types of districts.

Class size is often mentioned as an important determinant of both teacher retention and academic achievement. Texas made reducing class size a key element of educational reform in the 1980s and spent significant resources to achieve this end. The statewide stu-dent/teacher ratio dropped from 21:1 in 1980–81 to 15.6 in 1995–96, a 25 percent reduction in average class size. Class size in the average high-risk district is smaller than that in low-risk districts, as shown in Figure A.6. This is largely due to the higher proportion of special needs students who are generally taught in smaller classes.

Figure A.7 shows the proportions of district personnel who are teachers and teachers' aides, who could be considered instructional staff.[4] Although the three types of districts have about the same

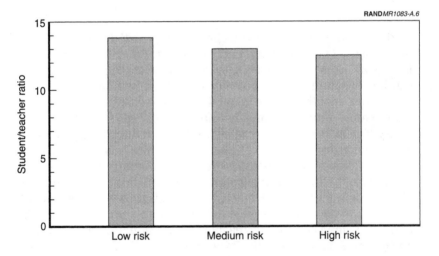

RAND*MR1083-A.6*

Figure A.6—Student/Teacher Ratios in Low-, Medium-, and High-Risk
Districts, 1995–96

---

[4]Other types of personnel are district or school administrative, professional support, and auxiliary staff. The proportions of staff in these categories are roughly even in the three types of districts.

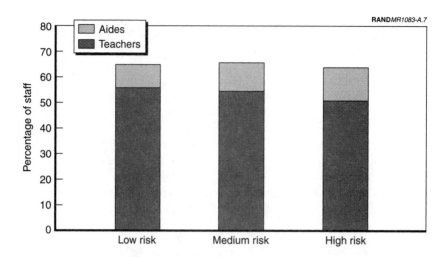

Figure A.7—Teachers and Aides as a Percentage of Total District Staff in Low-, Medium-, and High-Risk Districts, 1995–96

overall proportion of personnel working in classrooms, high-risk districts have more aides relative to teachers. There is at least one aide for every four teachers, whereas in low-risk districts there is less than one for every six teachers. Thus, somewhat surprisingly, in the average high-risk district, teachers have smaller classes and more aides. However, to conclude that this suggests that working conditions are somewhat better in high-risk districts would be both naïve and incorrect. We need to account for the very different student bodies served by the various districts; high- and medium-risk districts have much higher proportions of students needing remedial, special education, or bilingual classes. We also do not have a measure for school climate, school physical environment, and safety, all of which have a substantial effect on the ability to teach on the part of teachers and the ability to learn on the part of students.

RESULTS OF MULTIVARIATE MODELS BASED ON TEACHER CHARACTERISTICS, 1980–81 TO 1995–96

Table B.1

Means of Analysis Variables, 1980–81 to 1995–96

Characteristic	All	Non-Hispanic White	Hispanic	Black
Sample Size	152,814	119,545	22,123	10,002
Gender				
Female	0.76	0.78	0.72	0.73
Male	0.24	0.22	0.28	0.27
Age at entry				
20–24	0.32	0.34	0.24	0.21
25–29	0.35	0.34	0.39	0.35
30–34	0.12	0.11	0.15	0.16
35+	0.21	0.21	0.22	0.28
Degree				
BA	0.91	0.92	0.89	0.82
MA or Ph.D.	0.06	0.06	0.03	0.09
None	0.03	0.02	0.08	0.09
Primary teaching assignment				
Nondepartmental (elementary)	0.50	0.49	0.56	0.51
Special education	0.09	0.09	0.06	0.12
English	0.09	0.09	0.08	0.07
Mathematics	0.07	0.07	0.05	0.06
Physics/chemistry	0.004	0.004	0.002	0.002
Biology	0.02	0.02	0.02	0.02
Other departmental	0.23	0.23	0.23	0.22
Year of entry into teaching				
1980–1984	0.24	0.24	0.21	0.22
1985–1989	0.28	0.29	0.24	0.27
1990–1995	0.48	0.47	0.55	0.51
District educational risk				
Low	0.48	0.47	0.13	0.23
Medium	0.31	0.30	0.27	0.56
High	0.21	0.13	0.60	0.21
District community type				
Major urban	0.19	0.15	0.27	0.53
Other central city	0.14	0.12	0.25	0.10
Suburban fast growing	0.22	0.23	0.20	0.12
Suburban stable	0.18	0.20	0.09	0.12
Nonmetro with 1000+ ADA	0.15	0.16	0.13	0.09
Nonmetro with town	0.05	0.06	0.02	0.02
Rural	0.07	0.08	0.04	0.02
Race/ethnicity				
Non-Hispanic white	0.78			
Hispanic	0.14			
Black	0.07			

Table B.2
Multiplicative Factor Estimates for Cox Regression on Time to Attrition from Teaching, 1980–81 to 1995–96

Characteristic	All	Non-Hispanic White	Hispanic	Black
Gender				
Female	*1.0*	*1.0*	*1.0*	*1.0*
Male	0.965**	0.921**	1.035	1.199**
Age at entry				
20–24	*1.0*	*1.0*	*1.0*	*1.0*
25–29	0.840**	0.868**	0.794**	0.702**
30–34	0.713**	0.713**	0.770**	0.675**
35+	0.644**	0.617**	0.804**	0.675**
Degree				
BA	*1.0*	*1.0*	*1.0*	*1.0*
MA or Ph.D.	1.375**	1.373**	1.461**	1.307**
None	1.846**	1.529**	2.005**	2.434**
Primary teaching assignment				
Nondepartmental(elementary)	*1.0*	*1.0*	*1.0*	*1.0*
Special education	1.246**	1.237**	1.427**	1.217**
English	1.173**	1.166**	1.296**	1.208**
Mathematics	1.190**	1.182**	1.201**	1.493**
Physics/chemistry	1.404**	1.438**	1.471	1.189
Biology	1.154**	1.148**	1.256**	1.246*
Other departmental	1.080**	1.083**	1.153**	1.105*
Year of entry into teaching				
1980–1984	*1.0*	*1.0*	*1.0*	*1.0*
1985–1989	0.933**	0.889**	1.203**	1.138**
1990–1995	0.740**	0.693**	0.972	0.910*
District educational risk				
Low	*1.0*	*1.0*	*1.0*	*1.0*
Medium	1.059**	1.077**	0.985	1.019
High	1.107**	1.194**	0.865**	1.129*
District community type				
Major urban	1.171**	1.161**	1.105*	1.170**
Other central city	1.014	1.035*	0.907*	1.237**
Suburban fast growing	1.009	1.011	0.902*	1.191**
Suburban stable	*1.0*	*1.0*	*1.0*	*1.0*
Nonmetro with 1000+ ADA	0.940**	0.926**	0.939	1.130
Nonmetro with town	0.920**	0.905**	0.916	1.356**
Rural	1.001	0.989	1.074	1.184
Race/ethnicity				
Non-Hispanic white	*1.0*	—	—	—
Hispanic	0.754**	—	—	—
Black	0.868**	—	—	—

NOTE: For each variable, the omitted or reference group is given in italics.
* Significant at the .05 level.
**Significant at the .01 level.

Alston, D. A., *Recruiting Black Classroom Teachers: A National Challenge*, National Governors' Association, Washington, D.C., 1988.

Ball, D. L., and S. Wilson, "Becoming a Mathematics Teacher Through College-Based and Alternate Routes: The Relationship Between Knowing Your Subject and Learning to Teach It," paper presented at the annual meeting of the American Educational Research Association, Boston, Massachusetts, 1990.

Ballou, D., and M. Podgursky, "The Case Against Teacher Certification," *The Public Interest*, Vol. 132, 1998, pp. 17–29.

Berends, M., and D. Koretz, "Reporting Minority Students' Test Scores: How Well Can the NAEP Account for Differences in Social Context?" *Educational Assessment*, Vol. 3, No. 3, 1996.

Berends, M., and D. Koretz, *Identifying Students at Risk of Low Achievement in National Data*, RAND, Santa Monica, California, in press.

Bliss, T., "Alternate Certification in Connecticut: Reshaping the Profession," *Peabody Journal of Education*, Vol. 67, No. 3, 1990, pp. 35–54.

Choy, S. P., E. A. Medrich, and R. R. Henke, *Schools and Staffing in the United States: A Statistical Profile, 1987–88*, U.S. Department of Education, National Center for Education Statistics, Washington, D.C., 1992.

Cornett, L. M., "Alternate Certification: State Policies in the SREB States," *Peabody Journal of Education*, Vol. 67, No. 3, 1990, pp. 55–83.

Cox, D. R., "Regression Models and Life-Tables," *Journal of the Royal Statistical Society*, Series B 34, 1972, pp. 187–220.

Darling-Hammond, L., "Teaching and Knowledge: Policy Issues Posed by Alternate Certification for Teachers," *Peabody Journal of Education*, Vol. 67, No. 3, 1990, pp. 123–154.

Darling-Hammond, Linda, "The Current Status of Teaching and Teacher Development in the United States," background paper prepared for the National Commission on Teaching and America's Future, 1994.

Darling-Hammond, L., K. J. Pittman, and C. Ottinger, "Career Choices for Minorities: Who Will Teach?" paper presented for the National Education Association and Council of Chief State School Officers' Task Force on Minorities in Teaching, Washington, D.C., 1987.

Dilworth, M. E., "Teacher Testing: Adjustments for Schools, Colleges, and Departments of Education," *Journal of Negro Education*, Vol. 55, No. 3, 1986, pp. 368–378.

Dometrius, N. C., and L. Sigelman, "The Cost of Quality: Teacher Testing and Racial-Ethnic Representativeness in Public Education," *Social Science Quarterly*, Vol. 69, No. 1, 1988, pp. 70–82.

Ehrenberg, R. G., and D. J. Brewer, "Do School and Teacher Characteristics Matter? Evidence from *High School and Beyond*," *Economics of Education Review*, Vol. 13, No. 1, 1994, pp. 1–17.

Ehrenberg, R. G., and D. J. Brewer, *Did Teachers' Verbal Ability and Race Matter in the 1960s?* RAND, Santa Monica, California, 1995.

Ehrenberg, R. G., D. D. Goldhaber, and D. J. Brewer, *Do Teachers' Race, Gender, and Ethnicity Matter? Evidence from the National Educational Longitudinal Study of 1988*, RAND, Santa Monica, California, 1995.

Farrell, E. J., "On the Growing Shortage of Black and Hispanic Teachers," *English Journal*, Vol. 79, No. 1, 1990, pp. 39–46.

Feiman-Nemser, S., and M. Buchanan, "When Is Student Teaching Teacher Education?" *Teacher and Teacher Education*, Vol. 3, 1987, pp. 255–273.

Feistritzer, C. E., *Profile of Teachers in the U.S.—1990*, The National Center for Education Information, Washington, D.C., 1990.

Feistritzer, C. E., and D. Chester, *Alternative Teacher Certification: A State-by-State Analysis, 1998–99*, National Center for Education Information, Washington, D.C., 1998.

Fenstermacher, G. D., "The Place of Alternate Certificate in the Education of Teachers," *Peabody Journal of Education*, Vol. 67, No. 3, 1990, pp. 3–34.

Ferguson, Ronald F., "Racial Patterns in How School and Teacher Quality Affect Achievement and Earnings," *Challenge*, Vol. 2, No. 1, 1991, pp. 1–35.

Ferguson, Ronald, "Teachers Perceptions and Expectations and the Black-White Test Score Gap," in Christopher Jencks and Meredith Phillips (eds.), *The Black-White Test Score Gap*, Brookings Institution Press, Washington, D.C., 1998.

Fordham, S., and J. U. Ogbu, "Black Students' School Success: Coping with the 'Burden of Acting White,'" *The Urban Review*, Vol. 18, No. 3, 1986, pp. 176–206.

Gerald, D. E., and W. J. Hussar, *Projections of Education Statistics to 2007*, National Center for Education Statistics, Washington, D.C., 1997.

Goldhaber, Dan D., and Dominic J. Brewer, "Why Don't Schools and Teachers Seem to Matter? Assessing the Impact of Unobservables on Educational Productivity," *Journal of Human Resources*, Vol. 32, No. 3, 1997a, pp. 505–523.

Goldhaber, Dan D., and Dominic J. Brewer, "Evaluating the Effect of Teacher Degree Level on Educational Performance," in *Developments in School Finance, 1996*, National Center for Education

Statistics, U.S. Department of Education, Washington, D.C., 1997b.

Goldhaber, Dan D., Dominic J. Brewer, and Deborah J. Anderson, "A Three-Way Error Components Analysis of Educational Productivity," *Education Economics*, 1999.

Goldhaber, Dan D., and Dominic J. Brewer, *State Licensing and Student Achievement*, report from the Thomas B. Fordham Foundation, Washington, D.C., forthcoming.

Gomez, M. L., and T. Stoddart, "Learning to Teach Writing: The Balancing of Personal and Professional Perspectives," in R. Clift and C. Evertson (eds.), *Focal Points: Qualitative Inquiries into Teaching*, American Educational Research Association, Washington, D.C., 1991.

Grissmer, D. W., and S. N. Kirby, *Teacher Attrition: The Uphill Climb to Staff the Nation's Schools*, RAND, Santa Monica, California, 1987.

Grissmer, D. W., and S. N. Kirby, *Patterns of Attrition among Indiana Teachers, 1965–1987*, RAND, Santa Monica, California, 1992.

Grissmer, D. W., S. N. Kirby, M. Berends, and S. Williamson, *Student Achievement and the Changing American Family*, RAND, Santa Monica, California, 1994.

Grossman, P. L., "A Study in Contrast: Sources of Pedagogical Content Knowledge for Secondary English," *Journal of Teacher Education*, Vol. 40, No. 5, 1989a, pp. 24–31.

Grossman, P. L., "Learning to Teach Without Teacher Education," *Teachers College Record*, Vol. 91, No. 2, 1989b, pp. 191–208.

Haberman M., "The Rationale for Training Adults as Teachers," in C. Sleeter (ed.), *Empowerment Through Multicultural Education*, State University of New York, Buffalo, 1990.

Haggstrom, G. W., L. Darling-Hammond, and D. W. Grissmer, *Assessing Teacher Supply and Demand*, RAND, Santa Monica, California, 1988.

Hanushek, E. A., J. F. Kain, and S. G. Rivkin, "Teachers, Schools, and Academic Achievement," National Bureau of Economic Research, Working Paper 6691, 1998.

Hill, M. Ann, and June O'Neill, "Family Endowment and the Achievement of Young Children with Special Reference to the Underclass," *Journal of Human Resources,* Vol. 29, No. 4, 1994, pp. 1065–1100.

Holmes Group, *Tomorrow's Teachers: A Report of the Holmes Group,* East Lansing, Michigan, 1986.

Kalbfleisch, J. D., and R. L . Prentice, *The Statistical Analysis of Failure Time Data,* John Wiley and Sons, 1980.

Kearns, D., "Do Teachers Really Need Licenses?" *Wall Street Journal,* February 28, 1990, p. 14.

Kennedy, M. M., "Some Surprising Findings on How Teachers Learn to Teach," *Educational Leadership,* Vol. 49, No. 3, 1991, pp. 14–17.

Kerr, D. H., "Teaching Competency and Teacher Education in the United States," *Teachers College Record,* Vol. 81, No. 3, 1983, pp. 525–552.

Kirby, S. N., L. Darling-Hammond, and L. Hudson, "Nontraditional Recruits to Mathematics and Science Teaching," *Educational Evaluation and Policy Analysis,* Vol. 11, No. 3, Fall 1989, pp. 301–323.

Kirby, S. N., and L. Hudson, "Black Teachers in Indiana: A Potential Shortage?" *Educational Evaluation and Policy Analysis,* Vol. 15, No. 2, 1993, pp. 181–194.

Koretz, D., *Trends in the Postsecondary Enrollment of Minorities,* RAND, Santa Monica, California, 1990.

Kramer, R., "Ed School Follies: The Miseducation of America's Teachers," *The Free Press,* New York, 1991.

Lippman, L., S. Burns, and E. McArthur, *Urban Schools: The Challenge of Location and Poverty,* National Center for Education Statistics, Washington, D.C., 1996.

Ludwig, Meredith, and Laura Stapleton, *Sustaining the Supply of Math and Science Teachers: Assessing the Long-Term Effects of Nontraditional and Mid-Career Teacher Preparation Programs,* American Association of State Colleges and Universities, 1995.

Marquis, M. S., and S. N. Kirby, *Economic Factors in Reserve Attrition: Prior Service Individuals in the Army National Guard and Army Reserve,* RAND, Santa Monica, California, 1989.

McDiarmid, G. W., and S. M. Wilson, "An Exploration of the Subject Matter Knowledge of Alternate Route Teachers: Can We Assume They Know Their Subjects?" *Journal of Teacher Education,* Vol. 42, No. 2, 1991, pp. 93–103.

Monk, David, H., and Jennifer King, "Multi-Level Teacher Resource Effects on Pupil Performance in Secondary Mathematics and Science: The Role of Teacher Subject Matter Preparation," in Ronald G. Ehrenberg (ed.), *Contemporary Policy Issues: Choices and Consequences in Education,* ILR Press, Ithaca, New York, 1994.

Murnane, R. J., and B. R. Phillips, "Learning by Doing, Vintage, and Selection: Three Pieces of the Puzzle Relating Teaching Experience and Teaching Performance," *Economics of Education Review,* Vol. 1, No. 4, 1981a, pp. 453–465.

Murnane, R. J., and B. R. Phillips, "What Do Effective Teachers of Inner-City Chidren Have in Common?" *Social Science Research,* Vol. 10, 1981b, pp. 83–100.

Murnane, R. J., and M. Schwinden, "Race, Gender, and Opportunity: Supply and Demand for New Teachers in North Carolina, 1975–1985," *Educational Evaluation and Policy Analysis,* Vol. 11, No. 2, 1989, pp. 93–108.

Murnane, R. J., J. D. Singer, J. B. Willett, J. J. Kemple, and R. J. Olsen, *Who Will Teach? Policies That Matter,* Harvard University Press, Cambridge, Massachusetts, 1991.

National Commission on Teaching and America's Future, *What Matters Most: Teaching for America's Future,* Kutztown Publishing Co., Inc., Kutztown, Pennsylvania, 1996.

National Commission on Teaching and America's Future, *Doing What Matters Most: Investing in Quality Teaching*, Kutztown Publishing Co., Inc., Kutztown, Pennsylvania, 1997.

National Research Council, *The New Americans: Economic, Demographic, and Fiscal Effects of Immigration*, National Academy Press, Washington, D.C., 1997.

Natriello, G., E. L. McDill, and A. M. Pallas, *Schooling Disadvantaged Children: Racing Against Catastrophe*, Teachers College Press, New York, 1990.

Natriello, G., and K. Zumwalt, "New Teachers for Urban Schools? The Contribution of the Provisional Teacher Program in New Jersey," *Education and Urban Society*, Vol. 26, No. 1, 1993, pp. 49–62.

Ogbu, J., *The Next Generation: An Ethnography of Education in an Urban Neighborhood*, Academic Press, New York, 1974.

Ogbu, J., *Minority Education and Caste: The American System in Cross-Cultural Perspective*, Academic Press, New York, 1978.

Ogbu, J., "The Individual in Collective Adaptation: A Framework for Focusing on Academic Underperformance and Dropping Out Among Involuntary Minorities," in L. Weis, E. Farrar, and H. G. Petrie (eds.), *Dropouts from Schools: Issues, Dilemmas and Solutions*, State University of New York Press, Buffalo, New York, 1989, pp. 181–204.

Ogbu, J., "Understanding Cultural Diversity and Learning," *Educational Researcher*, Vol. 21, No. 8, 1992, pp. 5–14, 24.

Sanders, William L., and Sandra P. Horn, "The Tennessee Value-Added Assessment System (TVAAS): Mixed-Model Methodology in Educational Assessment," *Journal of Personnel Evaluation in Education*, Vol. 8, 1997, pp. 299–311.

Shen, J., "Has the Alternative Certification Policy Materialized Its Promise? A Comparison Between Traditionally and Alternatively Certified Teachers in Public Schools," *Educational Evaluation and Policy Analysis*, Vol. 19, No. 3, Fall 1997, pp. 276–283.

Shepard, Lorrie A., and Amelia E. Kreitzer, "The Texas Teacher Test," *Educational Researcher*, August–September, 1987, pp. 22–31.

Southern Regional Education Board (SREB), *Educator Supply and Demand in Texas: Report on Phase Two*, Atlanta, Georgia, 1996.

Spellman, S. O., "Recruitment of Black Teachers: Issues, Problems, Facts, Possible Solutions," *Journal of Teacher Education*, Vol. 39, No. 4, 1988, pp. 58–63.

State Board for Educator Certification (SBEC), *Who Is Teaching in Texas Public Schools?* Texas Education Agency, Austin, Texas, 1998.

Stoddard, T., "Learning to Teach English, Mathematics, and Science in an Alternative Route to Teacher Certification," *The Curriculum Journal*, Vol. 2, No. 3, 1991, pp. 259–281.

Stoddard, T., "The Los Angeles Unified School District Intern Program: Recruiting and Preparing Teachers for an Urban Context," *Peabody Journal of Education*, Vol. 67, No. 3, 1992, pp. 84–122.

Stoddard, T., and R. E. Floden, *Traditional and Alternative Routes to Teacher Certification: Issues, Assumptions, and Misconceptions*, Issue Paper 95-2, National Center for Research on Teacher Learning, East Lansing, Michigan, 1995.

Strauss, Robert P., and Elizabeth A. Sawyer, "Some New Evidence on Teacher and Student Competencies," *Economics of Education Review*, Vol. 5, No. 1, 1986, pp. 41–48.

Task Force on Teaching as a Profession, *A Nation Prepared: Teachers of the 21st Century*, Carnegie Forum on Education and the Economy, New York, 1986.

Texas Education Agency, *Texas Teacher Diversity and Recruitment: Report Number 4*, Austin, Texas, 1994.

Texas Education Agency, *Snapshot '95: 1994–95 School District Profiles*, Austin, Texas, 1995.

Texas Education Agency, *Snapshot '96: 1995–96 School District Profiles*, Austin, Texas, 1996a.

Texas Education Agency, *The Preparation and "Staying Power" of New Texas Teachers: Texas Teacher Preparation Study Final Report*, Austin, Texas, 1996b.

U.S. Bureau of the Census, *Statistical Abstract of the United States: 1995 (115th Edition)*, Washington, D.C., 1995.

U.S. Bureau of the Census, *Statistical Abstract of the United States: 1997 (117th Edition)*, Washington, D.C., 1997.

U.S Department of Education, National Center for Education Statistics, *Schools and Staffing in the United States: A Statistical Profile, 1993–94*, NCES 96-124, Washington, D.C., 1996.

U.S. Department of Education, National Center for Education Statistics, *America's Teachers: Profile of a Profession, 1993–94*, NCES 97-460, Washington, D.C., 1997.

Wilson, W. J., "Studying Inner-City Social Dislocations: The Challenge of Public Agenda Research," *American Sociological Review*, Vol. 56, 1991, pp. 1–14.

Zapata, J. T., "Early Identification and Recruitment of Hispanic Teacher Candidates," *Journal of Teacher Education*, Vol. 39, No. 1, 1988a, pp. 19–23.

Zapata, J. T., "Impact of Testing on Hispanic Teacher Candidates," *Teacher Education and Practice*, Vol. 4, No. 1, 1988b, pp. 19–24.

Zeichner, K., "The Practicum as an Occasion for Learning to Teach," *South Pacific Journal of Teacher Education*, Vol. 14, No. 2, 1986, pp. 11–298.